Chayil

JOHN ECKHARDT

Best-selling Author of *Prayers That Rout Demons*

CHARISMA
HOUSE

Most CHARISMA HOUSE BOOK GROUP products are available at special quantity discounts for bulk purchase for sales promotions, premiums, fund-raising, and educational needs. For details, write Charisma House Book Group, 600 Rinehart Road, Lake Mary, Florida 32746, or telephone (407) 333-0600.

CHAYIL by John Eckhardt
Published by Charisma House
Charisma Media/Charisma House Book Group
600 Rinehart Road
Lake Mary, Florida 32746
www.charismahouse.com

Unless otherwise noted, all Scripture quotations are taken from the King James Version of the Bible.

Scripture quotations marked AMPC are from the Amplified Bible, Classic Edition. Copyright © 1954, 1958, 1962, 1964, 1965, 1987 by The Lockman Foundation. Used by permission.

Scripture quotations marked ASV are from the American Standard Bible.

Scripture quotations marked DRA are from the Douay-Rheims 1899 American Edition of the Bible. Public domain.

Visit the author's website at www.johneckhardt.global.

Library of Congress Cataloging-in-Publication Data:
An application to register this book for cataloging has been
submitted to the Library of Congress.
International Standard Book Number: 978-1-62999-661-5
E-book ISBN: 978-1-62999-662-2

20 21 22 23 24 — 6 5 4 3 2
Printed in the United States of America

CONTENTS

CHAYIL–LOST in TRANSLATION

O N MOTHER'S DAY one year I preached a message titled "The Chayil Woman." The revelation connecting the Hebrew word *chayil* to women came as an answer to my prayer to the Lord for a word for mothers. So it happened that as I was studying, praying, and preparing, using the text we so often hear in church—Proverbs 31:10–31, I discovered something I had not seen before. The word *virtuous* in verse 10 is *chayil* in Hebrew. This word is commonly used in connection to men in terms of strength, wealth, and military might,[1] and I knew it well, as I had just finished a word study on *might*. I had looked up every scripture in the Bible on the word. Though it is translated different ways, it wasn't until I said, "Lord, I need a word for mothers and women," that the connection between the virtuous woman and *chayil* became clear.

Two verses in Proverbs use this word. One is Proverbs 12:4: "A virtuous woman is a crown to her husband, but she that maketh ashamed is rottenness in his bones." The other is Proverbs 31:10, as I mentioned, which reads, "Who can find a virtuous woman? for her price is far above rubies." Then there is yet another verse, Ruth 3:11: "And now, my daughter, fear not; I will do to thee all that thou requirest: for all the city of my people doth know that thou art a virtuous woman." Ruth is the only woman in the Bible to whom the word *chayil* is directly connected. What the Lord was showing me is that the virtuous woman *is* the chayil woman.

GETTING A MORE COMPLETE PICTURE
OF THE VIRTUOUS WOMAN

What's interesting about this revelation is that so many of us are familiar with the Proverbs 31 woman, the virtuous woman, yet our understanding of who this woman is has not been expressed in its fullness. Just looking at it on the surface, we gather that the passage is talking about all the things she does, and when we look up the word *virtuous*, we find that it means to be "morally excellent; righteous; chaste,"[2] good, to have high standards. It's basically a word that describes someone who is living holy, clean, and right. But just defining the word *virtuous* without looking into the original Hebrew word *chayil*, we miss out on capturing the full power and strength of this woman.

You may have heard the phrase *lost in translation* before. Sometimes when you translate a word from another language into English, the English language doesn't have a word that is an accurate or full description of all that the word entails in its original language. So the best we can do is use a word that is close enough to convey as much of the meaning as we can—though it never captures the fullness of that word.

An example of this is the Hebrew word *shalom*. It is translated as "peace" in the Bible, but *shalom* means much more than that. It means health, completeness, safety, welfare, and prosperity.[3] *Shalom* carries a much deeper meaning than what the English word *peace* conveys. Sometimes when you're studying the Scriptures, the Spirit of God will lead you to look up a word in the original Hebrew or Greek so that you can get a comprehensive understanding of the word's meaning.

The idea that the virtuous woman has high standards and strong morals, and is pure and of high quality, is true. But so much more about this woman can be seen when we break down her essence based on the full meaning of the Hebrew word *chayil*.

Isaiah 60:1 gives another view of this word. The chapter starts with "Arise, shine; for thy light is come, and the glory of the LORD is risen upon thee." If you read down through the verses and review the list of the attributes of glory, you'll see that one of the verses reads, "The forces of the Gentiles shall come unto thee" (v. 5). The word *forces* in this verse is *chayil*. It is translated as "forces" two times in Isaiah 60. The other instance is in verse 11. So we see that *chayil* means "forces" here but "virtuous" in Proverbs 12:4, 31:10, and Ruth 3:11. Same word, two different meanings. And there's more.

Chayil is translated fifty-six times as "army," thirty-seven times as "man of valor," twenty-nine times as a "host," fourteen times as "forces," thirteen times as "valiant," twelve times as "strength," eleven times as "riches," ten times as "wealth," nine times as "power," eight times as "substance," six times as "might," and five times as "strong."[4] By diving deeper into the Hebrew translation of the word *chayil*, we get a fuller and more expansive understanding that goes beyond the one word, *virtuous*.

LANGUAGE CHANGES OVER TIME

I have studied the word *might* or *chayil* for many years but had never seen it in connection with the virtuous woman. I soon discovered that others had used it.

I first heard the word when I was preaching in Toronto for Dr. Pat Francis. Through her teaching I found out that *chayil* represents wealth, power, and ability and is connected to wisdom. Her focus, it seemed at the time, was really on entrepreneurship, business, and being a chayil believer. What I later discovered is that she does make the connection between *chayil* and women. She says, "A chayil woman knows how to create and rule her world.... [This] Hebrew word for 'Dominion' means to tread down, to subdue; to crumble; to create; to make; to prevail against, to reign, to rule and to take. These are all active words that include taking the authority to defend what is yours (yourself, family, possessions, destiny) and to protect your personal prosperity and dignity."[5]

God blessed *both* man and woman and told them *both* to multiply, replenish, and subdue the earth (Gen. 1:28). He didn't just speak to the man to multiply, replenish, and subdue. Man and woman are to be corulers. The woman should rule alongside the man, which means we should have both strong men and strong women. It is not commonly taught that women are corulers with men. As a result, women have often taken a subservient role—sometimes because of religion and tradition—not even understanding the concept of headship and authority. Instead, erroneous teaching has them responding as if they are to do nothing and believing that man is solely responsible. But this chayil revelation shows us that it is God's plan for women to walk in power and dominion just as men do.

The overwhelming spread of this kind of teaching may have to do with the fact that the 1611 King James Version translators were all men. Katharine Bushnell wrote a book over a hundred years ago called *God's Word to Women*,[6] which offers a defense for women in ministry. Katharine studied Hebrew and Greek. In her studies, she notes that the King James Version of the Bible only translates the word *chayil* as "virtuous" one time, and it's in reference to women.

Historically the Anglican Church, out of which the King James translators came, did not allow for women preachers. They had priests, and all the priests were men. All the bishops were men. So their understanding was that women shouldn't preach. Even considering how the King James Version leaves the word *women* out of Psalm 68:11—"The

Lord gave the word: great was the company of those that published it"—it didn't surprise me that they would translate *chayil* as "virtuous."

Now, I don't want to destroy your faith in the King James Version. I use the King James. I love the King James. I memorize the King James. It's a great translation. However, it is a translation. And sometimes when you dig deeper into Scripture, you realize you can discover different things from translation to translation. I'm not throwing the King James Version out. Sometimes its archaic language can be more difficult to understand. And sometimes the meaning of words changes over time.

For example, the Book of James talks about a man "that weareth the gay clothing" (Jas. 2:3). The word *gay* here is not the same as how we use it today. In 1611 the word *gay* only meant to be happy. It meant colorful. Today it is used in reference to sexual orientation. Words do change, and this may be part of the reason we are seeing the King James Version's limited translation of *chayil* when used in reference to women.

THE MANY TRANSLATIONS OF *CHAYIL* THROUGHOUT SCRIPTURE

One of the things I love to do is take a word and study all the Scripture passages that use it. It helps to broaden and expand the meaning. In the King James Version and others *chayil* is translated as "virtuous." *Virtue* means power, strength, and inner quality.[7] The Latin word for *strength* is *virtus*, and it is from this that we get the word *virtue*.[8] Jesus felt virtue (power) leave His body when the woman with the issue of blood touched the hem of His garment. Let's take a look now at the various ways different Bible translations translate *chayil*.

Chayil means "valiant" or "valor."

Several Bible translations translate *chayil*, as found in Proverbs 31:10, as "valiant" or "valor."

> Who shall find a *valiant* woman? far and from the uttermost coasts is the price of her.
> —Proverbs 31:10, DRA, EMPHASIS ADDED

> Aleph Who can find a *valiant* woman? for her price is far above precious stones.
> —Proverbs 31:10, JUB, EMPHASIS ADDED

> Who can find an aishes chayil (a woman of *valor*, an excellent wife *Prov 12:4*)? For her worth is far above rubies.
> —Proverbs 31:10, OJB, EMPHASIS ADDED

> Who could ever find a wife like this one—she is a woman of strength and mighty *valor*! She's full of wealth and wisdom. The price paid for her was greater than many jewels.
> —Proverbs 31:10, TPT, EMPHASIS ADDED

Throughout Scripture *chayil* is translated with different words in the King James Version. Let's look at some verses that use those words.

Chayil means "wealth."

> But thou shalt remember the LORD thy God: for it is he that giveth thee power to get *wealth*, that he may establish his covenant which he sware unto thy fathers, as it is this day.
>
> —DEUTERONOMY 8:18, EMPHASIS ADDED

> And Naomi had a kinsman of her husband's, a mighty man of *wealth*, of the family of Elimelech; and his name was Boaz.
>
> —RUTH 2:1, EMPHASIS ADDED

Chayil means "substance."

> Bless, LORD, his *substance*, and accept the work of his hands: smite through the loins of them that rise against him, and of them that hate him, that they rise not again.
>
> —DEUTERONOMY 33:11, EMPHASIS ADDED

Chayil means "valor."

> So Joshua arose, and all the people of war, to go up against Ai: and Joshua chose out thirty

thousand mighty men of *valour*, and sent them away by night.

—JOSHUA 8:3, EMPHASIS ADDED

And the angel of the LORD appeared unto him, and said unto him, the LORD is with thee, thou mighty man of *valour*.

—JUDGES 6:12, EMPHASIS ADDED

Chayil means "strength."

The bows of the mighty men are broken, and they that stumbled are girded with *strength*.

—1 SAMUEL 2:4, EMPHASIS ADDED

For thou hast girded me with *strength* to battle: them that rose up against me hast thou subdued under me.

—2 SAMUEL 22:40, EMPHASIS ADDED

They go from *strength* to *strength*, every one of them in Zion appeareth before God.

—PSALM 84:7, EMPHASIS ADDED

Chayil means "power."

Now there was a man of Benjamin, whose name was Kish, the son of Abiel, the son of Zeror, the son of Bechorath, the son of Aphiah, a Benjamite, a mighty man of *power.*

—1 SAMUEL 9:1, EMPHASIS ADDED

Chayil means "host."

And he gathered an *host*, and smote the Amalekites, and delivered Israel out of the hands of them that spoiled them.

—1 SAMUEL 14:48, EMPHASIS ADDED

Chayil means "valiant."

And there was sore war against the Philistines all the days of Saul: and when Saul saw any strong man, or any *valiant* man, he took him unto him.

—1 SAMUEL 14:52, EMPHASIS ADDED

All the *valiant* men arose, and went all night, and took the body of Saul and the bodies of his sons from the wall of Bethshan, and came to Jabesh, and burnt them there.

—1 SAMUEL 31:12, EMPHASIS ADDED

Chayil means "train."

And she came to Jerusalem with a very great *train*, with camels that bare spices, and very much gold, and precious stones: and when she was come to Solomon, she communed with him of all that was in her heart.

—1 KINGS 10:2, EMPHASIS ADDED

Chayil means "army."

So these young men of the princes of the provinces came out of the city, and the *army* which followed them.

—1 KINGS 20:19, EMPHASIS ADDED

So I prophesied as he commanded me, and the breath came into them, and they lived, and stood up upon their feet, an exceeding great *army*.

—EZEKIEL 37:10, EMPHASIS ADDED

And the LORD shall utter his voice before his *army*: for his camp is very great: for he is strong that executeth his word: for the day of the LORD is great and very terrible; and who can abide it?

—JOEL 2:11, EMPHASIS ADDED

Chayil means "might."

And their brethren among all the families of Issachar were valiant men of *might*, reckoned in all by their genealogies fourscore and seven thousand.

—1 CHRONICLES 7:5, EMPHASIS ADDED

Chayil means "able."

> And their brethren, heads of the house of their fathers, a thousand and seven hundred and threescore; very *able* men for the work of the service of the house of God.
> —1 CHRONICLES 9:13, EMPHASIS ADDED

Chayil means "company."

> And when the queen of Sheba heard of the fame of Solomon, she came to prove Solomon with hard questions at Jerusalem, with a very great *company*, and camels that bare spices, and gold in abundance, and precious stones: and when she was come to Solomon, she communed with him of all that was in her heart.
> —2 CHRONICLES 9:1, EMPHASIS ADDED

Chayil means "war."

> Now after this he built a wall without the city of David, on the west side of Gihon, in the valley, even to the entering in at the fish gate, and compassed about Ophel, and raised it up a very great height, and put captains of *war* in all the fenced cities of Judah.
> —2 CHRONICLES 33:14, EMPHASIS ADDED

***Chayil* means "soldiers."**

> For I was ashamed to require of the king a band of *soldiers* and horsemen to help us against the enemy in the way: because we had spoken unto the king, saying, The hand of our God is upon all them for good that seek him; but his power and his wrath is against all them that forsake him.
>
> —Ezra 8:22, emphasis added

***Chayil* means "riches."**

> He hath swallowed down *riches*, and he shall vomit them up again: God shall cast them out of his belly.
>
> —Job 20:15, emphasis added

> But ye shall be named the Priests of the Lord: men shall call you the Ministers of our God: ye shall eat the *riches* of the Gentiles, and in their glory shall ye boast yourselves.
>
> —Isaiah 61:6, emphasis added

***Chayil* means "virtuous."**

> A *virtuous* woman is a crown to her husband: but she that maketh ashamed is as rottenness in his bones.
>
> —Proverbs 12:4, emphasis added

> Who can find a *virtuous* woman? for her price is far above rubies.
>
> —PROVERBS 31:10, EMPHASIS ADDED

> Many daughters have done *virtuously,* but thou excellest them all.
>
> —PROVERBS 31:29, EMPHASIS ADDED

Chayil means "forces."

> Then thou shalt see, and flow together, and thine heart shall fear, and be enlarged; because the abundance of the sea shall be converted unto thee, the *forces* of the Gentiles shall come unto thee.
>
> —ISAIAH 60:5, EMPHASIS ADDED

> Therefore thy gates shall be open continually; they shall not be shut day nor night; that men may bring unto thee the *forces* of the Gentiles, and that their kings may be brought.
>
> —ISAIAH 60:11, EMPHASIS ADDED

A GREAT COMPANY OF WOMEN

The more I studied this topic, the more I felt the Lord inspiring me to develop my findings and write a book on the chayil woman. What I discovered will bless, encourage, and launch women to be powerful and mighty in God.

We need more women preachers, ministers, prophets,

and apostles. We need more women in business, women of wealth, women who can pray and worship. We need more strong women to be empowered and promoted. As we'll discover, the chayil woman comes with a distinct and rare set of gifts and characteristics that needs to be activated in every sphere of society. We will see the kingdom of God increase exponentially when we allow women to return to their rightful place as the corulers God designed them to be.

I have a lot of strong spiritual daughters in the Lord. I've seen them go around the world, preaching to nations. They're taking teams. I don't believe in raising up weak daughters. I didn't raise my own daughter to be weak, run over, and dominated by a man. I raised her to be strong—and strong in discernment.

THE CHALLENGE

In June 2018 I posted a challenge on Facebook Live called "The Chayil Woman Challenge." For a little over a week I interviewed different women of God who are very strong women—Michelle McClain-Walters, Sophia Ruffin, Valora Shaw-Cole, Yolanda Stith, Pamela Hardy, Kendria Moore, and more. I have included in this book some of what they shared about their journeys to becoming chayil women.

These women are powerful spiritual warriors. They are strong in prayer and strong in worship. They are strong preachers and teachers. They are strong in the prophetic. These are chayil women. I believe you will be blessed to learn that they faced fears, opposition, traumatic pasts, failure and disappointment, and other challenges, but those challenges did not stop them from pursuing the calls of God on their lives.

WHY MEN NEED THIS BOOK

This message is not only for women but for men as well. Men, you need to know how to deal with a strong wife or woman and not be intimidated. Men need to learn not to beat up or beat down strong women. Let them be strong. As true chayil women, they will not dominate you or manipulate you. Proverbs 12:4 says, "A virtuous woman is a crown to her husband." And Proverbs 31:12 says, "She will do him good and not evil all the days of her life."

Manipulation, domineeringness, and control are witchcraft. These characteristics are part of the Jezebel spirit and most definitely *not* attributes of the strength and power of God flowing through godly women. We need our minds renewed in this area. Because of fear, men have held back chayil women, limited them, or used and abused them. For the men who have always made room for strong women, who have supported and promoted them, it's time to make sure all men see their high value and worth.

MY PRAYER FOR YOU

As you read this book, I pray that this word will ignite a spirit of might, power, and strength. I pray that a chayil anointing will come upon you. If you feel you've been a weak woman, just barely making it because of this or that, listen: it's not the will of God that men be the only strong ones in a society while women lag behind, weak and disappointed. No. Woman of God, the Lord wants you to rise up. I thank God for men, but your dependency is not on a man; it's on God. Trust the Lord.

You're not like other women. There is an anointing on you. You have the Spirit of God in you. You have the spirit of might and power. God never called you to be weak, to be fearful, or to pull back from warfare. God called you to be a valiant woman. He has called you to war in the spirit and win. He has anointed you to have victory after victory after victory.

My challenge to you is to allow the Lord to use you, whether it's through preaching, teaching, prophesying, deliverance ministry, prayer, intercession, business, entrepreneurship, or philanthropy and humanitarianism. Let yourself be as great a company as God would have you be. Don't be limited, diminished, or reduced by man. May you step out with confidence in your anointing as the chayil woman.

Chapter 1

A WOMAN of VALOR and MIGHT

IN OUR SOCIETY it is not uncommon to talk about strong women. Many of us have known strong women. Our mothers were or are strong—strong in character and power, whether it's spiritual strength, emotional strength, or otherwise. Most of us have known strong women of God who move in power, miracles, healing, and deliverance. They are full of the Holy Ghost. They are strong prayer warriors, intercessors, prophetesses, counselors, preachers, and teachers.

Yet somehow the enemy leads our first thoughts to men when it comes to might and valor. As we are discovering, however, the word *chayil* means wealth, substance, valor, strength, power, host, valiant, train, army, might, able, company, war, soldiers, riches, virtuous, and forces. And this word is used in connection with women as well as men.

Sometimes men are intimidated by strong women. And sometimes women say, "Well, I don't want to be too strong," without realizing that God created them to be strong. This kind of strength is not about physical strength or about women trying to be stronger than men. A lot of women have accepted the traditional definition of who a woman should be: She should be weak and stay in the kitchen. She should be quiet and not say anything.

Then God raises up women who become leaders—governmental, business, and church leaders. And people still say that a woman shouldn't even speak in church, that she should be silent. Society is now shifting to where women who at one time were not very visible in business are taking over in greater numbers in various leadership roles in certain industries.

Strong chayil women are not Jezebels. They are not overbearing and beating up on their husbands. But the virtuous woman is not just a nice woman who is holy, clean, and praised. She's a chayil woman who is also strong, mighty, and valiant.

Here's an interesting point: if you ever look up the name Sarah, or Sarai—Abraham's wife—you'll see that it is connected to her being "a mother of nations" (Gen. 17:16) and means "my princess" and "nobility."[1] The root word for the name Sarah is the Hebrew word *sar*, which literally means "ruler, leader, chief, official, head, and overseer."[2] It refers to someone of power. So Sarah, the woman of God, the woman of faith, was not just a wife who had a baby. She was a very powerful woman who was married to Abraham, a very powerful and wealthy man.

Deborah, a judge in Israel, was also a very powerful

woman. All of Israel came to her for sound judgment. Esther, a queen, was a very powerful woman too.

In Scripture we read of women who carried authority and were strong in prayer and worship. Of course in the Old Covenant you'll find more men walking in *chayil*. Still, God did not create women to be weak. And this is the problem: some men do not approve of strong women. They automatically call them Jezebels. Jezebel was a witch, a seductress—manipulative and domineering. Being a strong woman does not make you a Jezebel.

Both men and women should be strong. The Bible says, and this applies to women as well, "Be strong in the Lord, and in the power of his might" (Eph. 6:10). I pray that you would be strengthened with might by the Spirit in your inner being.

THERE'S NO JUNIOR HOLY GHOST FOR WOMEN

In the Scriptures men were the physical warriors, and kings fought many battles. Pharaoh had *chayil*. Moses had *chayil*. Joshua had *chayil*. David had *chayil*. Hezekiah had *chayil*. But women also had *chayil*. Women such as Esther, Deborah, Anna, Ruth, and Abigail had *chayil*. These were all women of influence and power.

These scriptures on might and power in Christ apply to women as well as men.

That he would grant you, according to the riches
of his glory, to be strengthened with might by
his Spirit in the inner man.

—EPHESIANS 3:16

Finally, my brethren, be strong in the Lord, and
in the power of his might.

—EPHESIANS 6:10

I can do all things through Christ which
strengtheneth me.

—PHILIPPIANS 4:13

When women receive the Holy Ghost, it's not the Holy
Ghost Jr. You have the same Holy Ghost that men have.
You can be strong, mighty, and powerful. You can walk
in wealth and business. You should be strong in the prophetic, in preaching, teaching, prayer, worship, or whatever
your call is. You should not become weak or reduce yourself
for the approval of men. You should not be dominated, run
over, or controlled. You are not to be a doormat for a man
or for a church. You should be strong.

This is who you are, chayil woman. I am challenging you
to be strong in the Lord and in what God has given you.
Walk in strength. Don't ever let culture or tradition make
you weak. You are not this "little woman" who is just run
over. No. You can have a quiet and meek spirit and still be
strong. As a matter of fact, the Bible talks about meekness as

a strength. It's a virtue. Let's go a little deeper into the fullness of the valor and might of the virtuous chayil woman.

WOMAN OF VALOR

In the Jewish culture Proverbs 31:10–31 is a poetic blessing husbands sing over their wives at the Sabbath table.[3] The term is *eshet chayil*, and it is a spontaneous blessing.

> Friends cheer one another on with the blessing, celebrating everything from promotions, to pregnancies, to acts of mercy and justice, and honoring everything from battles with cancer, to brave acts of vulnerability, to difficult choices, with a hearty "eshet chayil!"—woman of valor.
>
> So I set aside my to-do list and began using Proverbs 31 as it was meant to be used—not as yet another impossible standard by which to measure our perceived failures, but as a celebration of what we've already accomplished as women of valor.[4]

This changes the whole idea of Proverbs 31, which should now be liberating for women to read and not a reminder of who they are not.

Carol McCleod states:

> Materialism, physical beauty and creature comforts were never meant to be the substance of the life of a woman who was created for *chayil*!

You were created to help win this battle on planet earth!

You were created with power and with ability!

You were created to tap into the wealth of God on earth!

You were created to be a front-line warrior in the mighty army of God and for His purposes!

You were created to raise up the next generation of warriors for the kingdom of God!

You were created to take back real estate from the kingdom of darkness and to position yourself as an immovable proponent for all that is right and good.

You were created to pray for the sick with faith and with power.

You were created to use the resources that God has given to you as a treasure chest of generous giving and lavish investment in God's kingdom.

You were created, my sisters of the faith, to walk side by side with man, pushing back the darkness, subduing and taking dominion over the earth.

The fight was never intended to be man vs. woman; the battle was intended to be man and woman taking down strongholds and charging forward in victory against spiritual forces of wickedness.[5]

Kathi Woodall states:

> The Old Testament uses *chayil* most often in the
> context of war or battle. Traditionally, the role
> of a man is to fight for and defend his country
> or his homeland. Scripture is full of stories of
> the Israelite men leaving their homes to go to
> battle; over and over it refers to them as *chayil*.
> They are the valiant warriors who crossed the
> Jordan to claim the Promised Land and fought
> alongside Joshua. They were the "elite army" of
> Israel who could "wage war with great power" (2
> Chronicles 26:13). King David was *chayil* even
> before God chose him as king; he was "a mighty
> man of valor" (1 Samuel 9:1).
>
> These are merely a sampling of the imagery
> behind the word *chayil*. Like these valiant war-
> riors, a chayil woman fights for and defends her
> home. She protects it from invading negative
> influences and organizes those under her so that
> it runs smoothly and calmly. A chayil woman is
> strong, mighty, and efficient. She is valiant and
> virtuous. But, and this is a very important point,
> she is all of these things alongside her husband,
> never in opposition to him.[6]

Chayil women are women of valor.

As I mentioned, Ruth is the only woman in Scripture referred to directly with the word *chayil*. She is the woman of valor who surpassed them all.

Yael Ziegler states:

> Over the course of the narrative, Ruth is accorded various appellations, including: Moavite, shifkha, ama, woman, and daughter-in-law. Perhaps her most memorable designation is "eshet chayil," a woman of valor. Ruth is the only character in the Tanakh termed as such, and this accolade seems to be reserved for a truly ideal woman. The term chayil suggests Ruth's strength, integrity, loyalty, honesty, leadership, and efficiency. Although Boaz couches this appellation as the opinion of the people in the gate, it is Boaz who calls Ruth a woman of valor. It is therefore of particular significance that this description mirrors the one used about Boaz himself in Ruth 2:1. This equates Ruth with Boaz, suggesting that her behavior sets her on par with the venerable Judean leader. It also hints at their compatibility, and the possibility of creating a marriage between equals.[7]

Ruth becomes a woman of power and influence who is in the genealogy of Christ (Matt. 1:5).

Prophetess Michelle McClain-Walters wrote a book on

this called *The Ruth Anointing.*[8] I invited her to come and talk about this during my Chayil Woman Challenge on Facebook. She is another of my spiritual daughters who's been with me for almost thirty years. I've taught her everything I know, and she's taught me a lot as well. She is a strong prophet, preacher, and apostle. She is an author and a powerful prayer warrior. She is strong in activation, impartation, and deliverance. My ministry and my life have been blessed by being connected with her all these years. She and her husband, Floyd Walters Jr., preach and lead conferences around the country and the world. This is what the Lord has revealed to her about Ruth:

> When I think about the women in the Bible who had the characteristics of a chayil woman, I think of Ruth. I even believe, through my prophetic insight, that when Solomon wrote about the virtuous woman in Proverbs 31, he was writing about his great-grandmother, Ruth. She was the only woman in the Bible who was actually called a virtuous woman. In Ruth 3:11 Boaz said, "We all know you are a virtuous (or chayil) woman" [paraphrased].
>
> This means that Ruth had to have been doing something, something that was seen. By this, God showed me that chayil men recognize chayil women. God showed me that He is breaking the contention between men and women and He

is raising up Ruth and Boaz—chayil men and chayil women—and we are going to move forward together. The enemy has always tried to put us at odds. But I believe this is the set time where men and women will recognize that, yes, we are different, but we can walk in unity. In this regard, unity means that we are moving together, but we have a distinction. God wants us to understand that we are valuable because of our differences, not because of our sameness. Moving together in covenant as chayil women and chayil men is based on our valuing each other's differences. Though the enemy has caused us to fight against one another, I believe this is the time for chayil women and chayil men to walk together in unity. Together we defeat the powers of darkness.[9]

Chayil women are strong.

Women of God are intended to operate in might. Stella Payton states:

Chayil in its original framework is *eshet chayil* meaning woman of valor. Valor means great courage in the face of danger, especially in battle. It implies bravery and courage—doing what frightens you. Or pluck—the kind of daring that enables you to quickly remove someone from a dangerous or unpleasant situation. Chayil is nerve—braced mentally to face demanding situations. She is audacious—taking bold risks with confidence.

A chayil woman has backbone—strength of character, will and determination; spirit—energy with determination and assertiveness; and guts—personal courage with tough character, true grit—courage with resolve. She is a woman with moxie—force of character with determination and nerve. This is a true chayil woman. And these are the characteristics women need today.[10]

There is a great company (army) of chayil women who are declaring the Word.

> The Lord gave the word: great was the company of those that published it.
>
> —PSALM 68:11

> The Lord giveth the word: The women that publish the tidings are a great host.
>
> —PSALM 68:11, ASV

Some translations use the term *army*.

> The Lord gives the command [to take Canaan]; The women who proclaim the good news are a great host (army).
>
> —PSALM 68:11, AMP

The Lord provided the message. The women who proclaimed it were a great army.

—PSALM 68:11, EHV

The Lord gives the word; the women who announce the news are a great host.

—PSALM 68:11, ESV

The Lord gave matter to the women to tell of the great army.

—PSALM 68:11, GNV

Adonoi gave the word; rav (great) was the tzava (company, army) of the mevaserot (heralds, those that published it, the lady evangelists).

—PSALM 68:11, OJB

Chayil women are strong women in the Word. They are strong in prophesying. They are strong in decreeing and declaring. They are strong in confession.

God empowered women on the day of Pentecost. The daughters prophesied.

And it shall come to pass in the last days, saith God, I will pour out of my Spirit upon all flesh: and your sons and your *daughters* shall prophesy, and your young men shall see visions, and your old men shall dream dreams.

—ACTS 2:17, EMPHASIS ADDED

The Greek word *dunamis* means power, and this power comes through the Holy Spirit. Remember, women do not have the Holy Ghost Jr.

Scripture tells us that Philip had four daughters who prophesied.

> And the same man had four *daughters*, virgins, which did prophesy.
> —ACTS 21:9, EMPHASIS ADDED

BREAKING OUT OF THE BOX WITH SOPHIA RUFFIN

Chayil women prophesy. The word of the Lord is in their mouths. One of my spiritual daughters, Sophia Ruffin, was a guest on one of my Facebook Live Chayil Woman Challenge broadcasts where we discussed the chayil woman. She is a strong preacher who stepped out in ministry, traveling around the country. It takes a level of bravery, courage, and strength to step out and do what she's doing. We don't always encourage women to be bold, courageous, and brave because we're trying not to make them like men. But, as I've said, women should be brave and courageous, and many of them are despite the lack of encouragement in this area. So I asked Sophia, "How do bravery and courage fit in your life, in your testimony, and even your stepping into what you're doing today?" This is what she said:

> For years, you hear about the virtuous woman, and it sort of puts the woman in a box. Even

when you read it from our traditional perspective of Proverbs 31, it still feels like this woman is in a box. But it's [not] just about a *virtuous* woman. There is more to it. It's more about being brave, courageous, bold, full of valor, and coming through like a one-woman army. This new perspective that you are bringing out really brings this woman out [of] the box. You have brought more definition to her character. You have also brought more identity to the strength and power of a woman. It is powerful that we are no longer being secluded in this box of just being virtuous.

What I've learned is that you can still be a woman, still be feminine, while being brave and bold and a woman of war. I had a lot of challenges growing up, and as a woman, you have to carry a lot. The responsibility that's put on a woman, oftentimes at an early age, is a heavy load. Still, somehow you learn how to overcome. You learn how to walk through opposition. And so that's what this chayil woman revelation means to me.

I'm a courageous person. I'm bold because I didn't allow my life, my circumstances, the trials I had to go through, and all the things I had to overcome to stop me, block me, or sit me down. I chose to rise up. Yet when I rose up, I didn't rise up in my own strength. I rose up in the strength of God. When a woman has a relationship with God and she is able to rise in the strength of that, she becomes powerful. She becomes dangerous. She becomes confident. And she feels unstoppable

One of my things is keeping this mentality that when I see something that seems impossible, I'm the one who says, "I want that challenge. I want to be the one. I want to be the one to prove that it's possible." Many get timid. They shy away. They don't want to do it. But I grew up with this mentality. I grew up in overcoming. And like many women, when I become [sic] an adult and I was able to overcome and defeated the enemy multiple times, I became dangerous. Chayil women, we're dangerous.[11]

Boldness and courage

I have seen Sophia's boldness and courage. I've seen her launch out in ministry and travel around the country. And what I love about Sophia is this: when it comes to courage, she has an abundance. She had the courage to tell her testimony. A lot of people are ashamed of their testimony, but because she had the courage to share it, thousands have been set free. She even wrote a book about it called *Set Free and Delivered: Strategies and Prayers to Maintain Deliverance.*[12] She says,

Before anybody knew my name and before I had any of these opportunities or a platform, I spent eight years in the wilderness walking out my deliverance and getting free from homosexuality, giving me the ability to trust God and believe that it is possible to get free and stay free. This is what I wrote about in my book. I also talk about being proactive in spiritual warfare. You can be victorious and courageous. You can't always be reactive. But you've got to be proactive. That's the thing about a chayil woman: she knows that she can't always be reactive and that she must not always wait on a situation to happen and then respond to it. You have to be proactive in spiritual warfare and know how to destroy the enemy before he is able to attack you. That's what I love about strong, confident women, women of power who say, "This is what I went through, but this is how I made it out." We are a voice of hope for somebody else who may be in that same struggle and who may be waiting on somebody to be bold enough, courageous enough to share their testimony.

I said, "OK, God, if You're going to use anybody, then use me." So I just started with being bold. Once I shared my testimony and being a hope for many people to say, "Wow, God did it for you; He can do it for me." And that's when I just began to write books.

And I stay in my lane. I use discernment when different situations come up. For some of them, I think, "OK, shame comes with that."

A lot of people are sitting on their power, sitting on their anointing, sitting on their deliverance, and sitting on somebody else's breakthrough because they allowed the demon called shame to shut them up. But I believe God is raising up courageous women who will talk and testify about what they've overcome and how they made it out. When God adds His anointing on top of that, oh, you're powerful!

So I just walk in the strength of my identity. God is with me, and I am unshakable. I'm not intimidated by the enemy.[13]

It took courage for Sophia to step out the way she has. It took valor. And that's what *chayil* means. It means courageous, valor, valiant. Sophia and other chayil women like her are strong preachers who give it all they have. Oftentimes women have been told they can't preach. But chayil women preach with the strength and power of God, despite opposition. Men get delivered under their ministry. Women get delivered. Young people get delivered. The chayil woman is a blessing to all those she ministers to. Chayil women don't just do women's meetings. They cast out devils and prophesy with the full power of the Holy Ghost.

I am challenging you, woman of God, to rise up and be strong, just as I would any of my spiritual daughters. Don't be a weak woman. Don't be timid. Don't be fearful. Don't be ashamed. Don't hide. Don't draw back. Don't let people tell you that you can't do it because you're a woman. Don't feel as if you're a second-class citizen. In Christ there is neither male nor female. The Bible says that both sons *and* daughters will prophesy. There is a place for you.

VALOR IS MY NAME WITH VALORA SHAW-COLE

Valora Shaw-Cole and her husband, LaJun Cole, pastor Contagious Church in Tampa, Florida. She is a spiritual daughter and a powerful prayer warrior and preacher. I've had her open up our conferences in prayer. Not only does Valora serve actively in ministry, but she has an impact in the school system and her local government. She has also written several books.

The reason I invited her to join me on my Facebook Live Chayil Woman Challenge in June 2018 is that her name is Valora. I never saw that the word *valor* is in her name until I did this chayil challenge. So I asked her to share about her name, how she came to understand it, the power behind it, and what a revelation of her name has done for her life. This is what she said:

For years I certainly didn't know who I was. I remember God asking me twenty years ago, "What does [your] name mean?" I had no idea. I was going through a very challenging time in my life, so I began to study the Word. I heard God say, "Look up *valor*." When I did, I saw that it meant to be bold, to be strong, and to be courageous.

I said, "Well, wow, God. This is what You're telling me? I have to be bold? I have to be strong? I have to be courageous?"

I was a nurse at that time, and I had to write my name several times a day. God said to me, "Every time you write your name, every time you speak your name, every time your name is spoken, a declaration is being made about who you are."

This revelation really caused me to dig deeper. For so many years I was told that I was nothing, that I was no good, that I would never amount to anything, that I would never do anything, and no one would ever love me. This is what I grew up believing in my own home. When I went to school, I was bullied by my peers. Being ostracized so much and in this way, I felt as though I had no worth or value when it came to anything. I allowed fear to actually silence me. I allowed fear to paralyze me. I grew up very fearful and intimidated. I had a fear of rejection and a fear of success. And I did well in school. I always excelled. I was on the dean's list. But even those things caused me to be rejected. Excelling caused me to be rejected. I felt like I was in this place where I didn't know what to do.

So I began to search the Word, and God began to deal with me and show me who I really was. He showed me that I was fearfully and wonderfully made, that I was created in His likeness and in His image, and that He knew me before I was in my mother's womb. But even with my conception, I had adverse situations. My mother was not married to my father at the time, and it was a very challenging time for her.

I didn't know my father. I only knew his name. It wasn't until I was in my early twenties that I met him. So part of me felt this emptiness because I didn't know and didn't understand. My mother and I were so different. I felt like I was in a family I didn't belong in. I went through that whole process of healing. Went through the process of renewing my mind. And it was so key for me. God said to me, "You must renew your mind. You must read My Word. You must continue to confess who you are according to My Word. You must know the truth, because the enemy will always show you something that is not the truth. He'll even show you the facts, but you must understand the truth."[14]

What Valora has come through and how she is doing all that she's doing, and has done both professionally and in the ministry, demonstrate her testimony of moving forward in valor, courage, and boldness. God has this same path outlined for all His chayil women—to take them from who others have told them they are to a place of strength, might, and power. There are several instances in the Bible where God made His truth about a person's identity clear by giving the person a new name—Abram to Abraham, Sarai to Sarah, Jacob to Israel, Saul to Paul, and so on. You may not get a new name in the natural, but God wants to make you aware of what, or rather *who*, He calls you. Are you fearful or faith-filled, timid or bold, doubtful or trusting, rejected or accepted, soft-spoken or outspoken? Who is God calling you in this season? What is your name?

Chapter 2

A WOMAN of WISDOM
and DISCERNMENT

O NE OF THE verses I keep mentioning is Psalm 68:11: "The Lord gave the word. Great was the company of those that published it." In the Hebrew the verse actually reads, "Great was the company of *women* who published it." The King James Version took out the word *women*. If you look at other translations, some say, "Great was the company of women who published it." There have been so many situations where women were told they can't preach, can't teach, and are not called. And yet God says, "When I give the word, I am going to raise up a great company of women who will proclaim the word."

One of the central characteristics of a chayil woman is her ability to hear from God and deliver His word through wise actions, discernment, and godly counsel. Chayil women prophesy, encourage, edify, build up, and bring wisdom into any situation or place God sends them to. In their homes, churches, and businesses, chayil women's presence is a benefit to all those who welcome and promote their gifts.

ABIGAIL, A CHAYIL WOMAN OF WISDOM

Abigail is one of my favorite chayil women in Scripture. She had the wisdom to approach King David when he was coming to kill her entire family because of her husband's foolishness.

> Then Abigail made haste, and took two hundred loaves, and two bottles of wine, and five sheep ready dressed, and five measures of parched corn, and an hundred clusters of raisins, and two hundred cakes of figs, and laid them on asses.
>
> —1 SAMUEL 25:18

David commended Abigail for her wisdom. After her husband's death, Abigail married the king. Her marriage to the king was due to her beauty and wisdom. She became an influential woman in Israel by her marriage to the king.

THE LADY OF WISDOM

Wisdom is described as a lady in the Book of Proverbs. In Proverbs 1:20–33 and 8:1–9:12 wisdom is personified as a woman who has much to offer—including "enduring wealth and prosperity" and "life"—to anyone who would heed her words (8:18, 35). Wisdom gives strength.

Counsel is mine, and sound wisdom: I am understanding; I have strength.

> —PROVERBS 8:14

And all the women that were wise hearted did spin with their hands, and brought that which they had spun, both of blue, and of purple, and of scarlet, and of fine linen.

> —EXODUS 35:25

She layeth her hands to the spindle, and her hands hold the distaff.

> —PROVERBS 31:19

Wisdom is connected to strength.

With him is wisdom and strength, he hath counsel and understanding.

> —JOB 12:13

Behold, God is mighty, and despiseth not any: he is mighty in strength and wisdom.

> —JOB 36:5

Wisdom is connected to might.

And the spirit of the LORD shall rest upon him, the spirit of wisdom and understanding, the spirit of counsel and might, the spirit of knowledge and of the fear of the LORD.

—ISAIAH 11:2

Daniel answered and said, Blessed be the name of God for ever and ever: for wisdom and might are his.

—DANIEL 2:20

I thank thee, and praise thee, O thou God of my fathers, who hast given me wisdom and might, and hast made known unto me now what we desired of thee: for thou hast now made known unto us the king's matter.

—DANIEL 2:23

And when he was come into his own country, he taught them in their synagogue, insomuch that they were astonished, and said, Whence hath this man this wisdom, and these mighty works?

—MATTHEW 13:54

DEBORAH, A CHAYIL WOMAN OF DISCERNMENT AND COUNSEL

Deborah is one of the most amazing chayil women in Scripture. She was a judge in Israel and also a prophetess.

And the children of Israel cried unto the LORD:
for he had nine hundred chariots of iron; and
twenty years he mightily oppressed the children
of Israel.

And Deborah, a prophetess, the wife of
Lapidoth, she judged Israel at that time.

And she dwelt under the palm tree of Deborah
between Ramah and Bethel in mount Ephraim:
and the children of Israel came up to her for
judgment.

—JUDGES 4:3–5

Deborah had wisdom and discernment to judge. She was
a seer who judged an entire nation.

By her example we see that chayil women issue verdicts
and pass judgments.

A great encourager

Deborah went up against the enemy with Barak, the military commander of Israel. She encouraged Barak to fight.

And she said, I will surely go with thee: notwithstanding the journey that thou takest shall
not be for thine honour; for the LORD shall sell
Sisera into the hand of a woman. And Deborah
arose, and went with Barak to Kedesh.

—JUDGES 4:9

And Deborah said unto Barak, Up; for this is the day in which the LORD hath delivered Sisera into thine hand: is not the LORD gone out before thee? So Barak went down from mount Tabor, and ten thousand men after him.

—JUDGES 4:14

SPEAKING RIGHT WORDS AND THE LAW OF KINDNESS WITH MICHELLE MCCLAIN-WALTERS

Read what Michelle McClain-Walters has to say about the words of a chayil woman. As a woman of God, you are called to speak "right words":

As a chayil woman, you have a special grace. Proverbs 31:26 says, "The law of kindness is in her mouth." There is something in your words. Woman of God, we have an ability to speak right words that call a nation to arise, that call a general to his destiny, and that cause a nation to arise and fight for the principles of God.

Let's consider Deborah's position. Her position as judge was equivalent to a president in our day. Looking across all those who held the position of judge in ancient Israel, notice that Samson fought with the jawbone of a donkey (Judges 15:15–16). Ehud, the left-handed man, used a dagger (Judges 3:15–16). But guess what

Deborah's weapon was? Words. God said, "I will put the words in her mouth."

Chayil women stand in the counsel of the Lord. We mark and we perceive His words. God will give you a word. He will cause you to speak to women, men, and even situations. All chayil women have a prophetic dimension on our lives. You have the spirit of counsel.

Deborah had counsel, and she had might. God will put the counsel in your spirit, because you have prophetic grace to see, to hear, to know the strategy and the plan of God. Then He will give you the spirit of might. See, *chayil* means might. *Might* is the impetus, the force, to carry out the counsel of God.

Deborah said the right words at the right time that mobilized an entire nation. Her war weapon was her words. Chayil women are women who speak mighty words. We are women of valor. We have the right words, and as the verse says, the law of kindness is in our mouths.[1]

CONFIRMING THE WORD OF THE LORD WITH KENDRIA MOORE

When I did the Chayil Woman Challenge, it brought to mind so many women of God I know. Many of them are spiritual daughters, women who have prophesied for years with me, going around the world to different nations prophesying. Through them I've seen the word of the Lord bring deliverance and healing and do so many miraculous things. I encourage my spiritual daughters to be strong in the prophetic. It is so important.

For Kendria Moore, the prophetic is something she lives for. God is using her in her Houston ministry to stir up other women who have the same testimony she has—"nobodies," people who were rejected, overlooked, and told they would never be anything. She uses impartation, prophesying, teaching, training, praying, and worshipping to get them activated and flowing in the power of God. I asked her to share her testimony and what it has been like to serve as a prophetic chayil woman. Here's what she told me:

> I started my ministry in 2013, and to be honest with you, ministry wasn't what I wanted to do. I had so many other visions and dreams, and one day the Holy Spirit was speaking to me, and I knew it was time.
>
> It all started years ago when Dr. Juanita Bynum prophesied to me that God had some big things for me—things that I was going to do and that I had special gifts [for]. Years later, in 2013, God connected us by way of confirmation. We had the same vision. I heard God say that He was going to use me to get the body of Christ back to the place where He first called them,

back to their first love. Then He used Dr. Bynum to tell me to host a conference.

I had never run a revival before. I never had put on any type of event. But God said to me, "You can do it." I was a nobody. I wasn't somebody people knew. I was just this person minding their business, a single mother.

I birthed my first conference, and it was powerful. It was a healing and deliverance conference in Houston, Texas. People came from all over the world. We had over one thousand people who came to be a part of that great move of God. It was so powerful that we ended up staying in the church overnight. We went in Friday night and didn't come out until late Saturday afternoon. God moved like crazy. It was prayer like no other. We had a midnight prayer.

From that God continued to birth out conferences, and He gave me the ministry Prophetic Flow Ministries. I believe that Prophetic Flow Ministries is symbolic of the prophetic call that is on my life. God has called me into the gift of prophecy as a mouth gate to speak His word. And when I speak His word, I believe that something happens, and people get healed, delivered, and set free. I didn't even know there was an anointing on my life like there was, but [what]

I've found is that the people who didn't want it are the people He is using.

This wasn't what I wanted, but now that I'm doing it, this is all that I know. I don't know anything else but to speak life into people. I don't know anything else but to decree and declare healing over people's lives. I don't want anything else. This is what I breathe. It's what I live. It's what I love—day in and day out.[2]

The ostracized, the pushed aside, the nobodies

I asked Kendria to talk about why she felt the prophetic gift for the chayil woman was important. This is what she said:

A lot of people don't even know that I was labeled as a little girl, and I was told that I would never be anything. And I believe that this is a part of the ministry. God is sending people to this ministry who have been labeled, who have been ostracized, and who have been pushed to the side, the nobodies, the ones who have been told they cannot go forward. By my being labeled, being in special ed, and just being a little girl who went through so much tragedy as a kid, God allowed me to birth this ministry out now. I didn't understand the trials then, but I know now that they were for His glory. And so

I celebrate today after five years in ministry, and God is doing the unheard of.

I've seen so much in this prophetic walk, one that I'd like to call a death walk, if I can say. Experiencing the prophetic, for me, God has just opened my eyes to all kinds of blessings and situations and miracles and testimonies.

I remember this one time, I was at a service being held in a ballroom of a hotel and felt as if I was choking, so I went to the bar. (I heard, "Go to the bar," so I went.) When I got to the bar, I asked the bartender if I could please get some water to drink. As I was drinking the water, the Holy Spirit led me over to a young lady who was sitting to my right, and I looked at her. I began to tell her that God said that He wanted to heal her. I didn't know the girl. I said, "God said He is going to heal everything that you've been dealing with, everything that you've been going through." I began to prophesy to this stranger.

As I prophesied to this young girl, she was taking shots of this drink. She was drinking a whole lot of liquor at the time. She looked at me and said, "I don't even know you, but what you don't know is that I was on the verge of committing suicide before you came and said something to me." She said, "I was on the verge of literally taking my life. But your words have encouraged me; your words let me know that there is a God, and God is for real."

Then she compared me to her grandmother. She said, "I never thought I would meet anybody who was spiritual like my grandmother." That night she did not kill herself but instead gave her life to Christ.

Afterward God said, "The reason why I sent you to get water is because water represents life. I caused your throat to burn because she was going to hang herself in the hotel room. I allowed you to experience what she was going to experience."[3]

Chayil women are mouth gates.

Kendria continued:

I believe this represents the importance of the chayil woman who is gifted prophetically. It's so important that we are keen, that we have keen ears and we are listening for what God is saying because you never know if it is a life-or-death situation. You never know who needs what God is saying.

I believe that prophets are mouth gates. They come to comfort. They come to exhort. They come to give the word of God, and it's so important because people are depending on the word of God. They are depending on God's voice.

It's not always death situations. There are some people who are depending on you to tell them that God is about to promote them. Promotion is great because it gives them that faith, understanding that if God said it, it's final. If God said it, then He's going to do it. And many times this is a confirming word for what the person already has some knowledge of.

I believe that God called me to confirm. I am a confirmation prophet. Whatever God speaks to me, it's always confirming what the person already knows. So He's not going to use me to tell them something they don't know. He uses me to confirm something He's already spoken, something that already resonates with their spirit.[4]

Thousands of women, like Kendria, are preaching, teaching, prophesying, and casting out devils. These are amazing times. Sometimes people look at the church and say, "I don't see the power. Where's the power?" If you don't see any power, you're in the wrong place. God is using a lot of ministries, especially those led by chayil women, to perform the miraculous on a consistent basis.

For those who say they don't see the kind of power that was present in the Book of Acts, I don't know what church you're going to or whom you've been hanging around. There is more happening today than at any other time in history.

There are more prophets, more prophetic words, more miracles, and more deliverances today than at any other time in history. The work that Kendria and many others do, traveling from city to city and nation to nation, shows the power of God to this generation and the next. Every generation needs to see the power of God. Chayil women have a part to play in releasing the power—the signs, wonders, and miracles—of God to this particular generation.

Chapter 3

A WOMAN of SUBSTANCE and WEALTH

THE CHAYIL WOMAN is a wealthy woman. The Bible says this in Deuteronomy 8:18:

> But thou shalt remember the LORD thy God: for it is he that giveth thee power to get wealth, that he may establish his covenant which he sware unto thy fathers, as it is this day.

The word "wealth" is *chayil*.[1] The chayil woman has force. She has power. She's not just a normal woman. She is virtuous. She's chayil. She knows how to handle money. She knows how to handle her business. Don't you ever feel bad about handling your business. Say it with me right now: "I handle my business. I have chayil in my life. I have the strength of God in my life." If you don't handle your business, somebody else will. And nobody can handle your business better than you can.

You can own property. You can own land. You can have money in the bank. You can have investments. You can have financial strength. You can be on boards. You can be on committees. You can have your own foundation. You can own trusts. You can be in the stock market. You can handle your business as a woman. Don't limit yourself. For some who believe that their only way to wealth is by marrying a man who has money, know that you have within you the power to be wealthy too. There's nothing wrong with marrying someone who's wealthy. The point here is to not limit your own abilities to walk in the wealth and might of chayil.

THE CHAYIL WOMAN IS A FINANCIAL FORCE

As we've pointed out, *chayil* means riches. When you're wealthy, you have financial force or financial strength. Chayil means wealth, power, forces, and armies. So when it says in Isaiah 60:11 that the army, or the forces, of the Gentiles and their kings will be brought to Zion, what it's saying is that when the kingdom and the glory come, then the wealth, strength, and power of the Gentiles shall come to Zion.

When you arise and shine, because your light has come, as Isaiah 60:11 says, the Gentiles shall come. And they come bringing their talents, their strength, their wealth, their power, and their forces to Zion.

God wants you wealthy. You don't have to be broke. You're a virtuous woman. You're a chayil woman. As you continue to read and pray through Proverbs 31:10–31, you will see that she is a businesswoman. She finds a field and buys it. God wants women to be businesspeople.

CHAYIL, EFFICIENCY, AND WEALTH

What I found even more interesting about *chayil* is that, according to *Strong's Exhaustive Concordance*, the word is also connected to efficiency.[2] To be efficient means to achieve "maximum productivity with minimum wasted effort or expense."[3] This means that if you're going to be chayil, you can't waste your time on some stuff. I'll say it like this: don't waste your time on people and things that are not productive. The chayil woman is an efficient woman.

Some of us had mothers who were so efficient. They knew how to get the most out of a little. They were efficient in the house. They were efficient with clothing. They were efficient with money. They were efficient with food. They knew how to take a little and stretch it far. Because they weren't just any women; they were chayil women. They had a strength about them, even though they didn't have much.

You know, many of us grew up in a house where the phone was never cut off. Today folks' phones are always off. Back then people knew how to pay the phone bill. The gas bill. The rent. Put food on the table. Even though you may have felt as if you were poor, you always had food. You were never hungry, because you had a woman in the house who knew how to be efficient. That's why I love chayil women.

Say this with me now: "Make me efficient, Lord."

Some of us waste too much time on stuff that's not important or productive. You waste your life hanging out with losers, bottom-feeders, and people who suck you dry. When it's all over, you have nothing.

But not for the chayil woman. She is an efficient woman. She knows how to use her time. She knows how to use her schedule. She knows how to get something done. She doesn't waste her time on frivolous things. She doesn't waste her time gossiping and hanging out with vain people. She doesn't waste her time in the club. She doesn't waste her time doing things that don't bring blessing, things that don't bring breakthrough.

She's a virtuous woman. She's an efficient woman. She says: "I don't have time for that. I don't have time to hang out with you if you aren't doing anything. I don't have time to chase a man all over the place. I don't have time to be with a different man every time you look. I'm not wasting my life or my time. I don't have time to have ten babies by ten baby daddies. I don't have time for that. I have better ways to use my time than by sleeping around with every loser in town." The chayil woman is the one you'll hear say, "Ain't nobody got time for that."

She's too busy doing things that matter. She's too busy living a life that is productive. She trusts God. She doesn't need a sugar daddy. She is efficient and doesn't waste herself, her gifts, talents, mind, emotions, resources, or body on anyone or anything that is not profitable to her movement in life.

The chayil woman is business-minded. She is competent, productive, capable, and organized.

God is raising up businesswomen, women in the marketplace who can go out there and make money and be blessed, women who can release a product that meets needs and solves problems. The chayil woman's excuse is not, "I'm a woman, and I can't do this." No. She makes no excuses, and being confident in who God made her to be, she says, "I can do this because I am a woman—a virtuous woman, God's woman, a chayil woman."

CHAYIL, WEALTH, AND MALE-DOMINATED SOCIETY

It should not be uncommon or unusual to find wealthy women. Society sometimes has made it difficult for women to advance and break through. Sometimes women have gone into the marketplace and been dealt with in a sexual way. And they've been attacked sexually—you know the story. In Hollywood bad behavior is finally being exposed. For much of it, we knew what was going on the whole time, where women are forced into sex in exchange for leading roles. But God says to you, woman, "I've created you to be a virtuous woman. I created you to be a chayil woman. I did not create you to be a doormat or to be controlled, abused, taken advantage of, molested, run down, or ignored. I created you to be efficient, wealthy, strong, and powerful."

It's a wonderful thing when a woman steps into her moment of favor and everybody says, "Wow! Where did she come from?" But they don't know her Daddy.

WEALTH AND MIGHT

Might is the ability to do things you ordinarily could not do. Might means that you have strength to break through walls, barriers, and opposition. The devil loves to put walls around women and hinder their progress. He hates women because it was the seed of a woman that bruised his head. (See Genesis 3:15.) He wants to keep women in a place where they don't feel strong. And if there's a point when they become strong, men sometimes say, "Well, who do you think you are?" because men have too often looked at women as sex objects, thinking and behaving as if to say, "You're here for my pleasure." Men don't expect women to be billionaires—until Oprah showed up. I like that: billionaire women right in front of everybody.

How is it that we can see these breakthroughs, then sit back and say, "Oh, that's nice," but don't believe they can happen in our lives? Woman of God, are you believing for this level of breakthrough in your life? Are you believing for the spirit of might?

Might gives you the ability to get wealth. There is a certain strength you must have to become wealthy. You have to break through some stuff. You have to overcome some stuff. You have to deal with some challenges. You have to deal with some demons that have been determined to keep you bound and from fulfilling your dreams. You have to deal with some business demons called thieves and liars. God will give you the spirit of might to do it. He will give you the ability to make the right decisions, to get discernment, to look out for the snakes, and to break through.

It will be that when the bank says no, God says yes. When

they say you can't do that, you'll say, "My product will hit the market. I will break through. I will be a success."

The spirit of might doesn't empower you to do everything the way a man would. Women are women, and men are men. We were created with differences in the way we express strength. Just because you're a woman doesn't mean you have to be weak, nor does it mean you have to get out there stumping like the big dogs. In other words, you don't have to turn into a man to see the spirit of might come upon you and give you power to get wealth and be successful in business. Women in business have unique strengths that should not be overwritten by male-dominated beliefs.

Chayil women are women of substance.

Remember, this word means riches, wealth, and substance. Chayil women are givers.

> And certain women, which had been healed of evil spirits and infirmities, Mary called Magdalene, out of whom went seven devils, and Joanna the wife of Chuza Herod's steward, and Susanna, and many others, which ministered unto him of their substance.
>
> —LUKE 8:2–3

These women, who had been healed and delivered from infirmities and demons, ministered to Christ of their substance. They supported Jesus' ministry. Chayil women are healed and delivered women.

61

Chayil women are entrepreneurial.

They know how to handle real estate and property. The daughters of Zelophehad requested their inheritance after the men had died in their family. God told Moses to give them their request.

> The daughters of Zelophehad speak right: thou shalt surely give them a possession of an inheritance among their father's brethren; and thou shalt cause the inheritance of their father to pass unto them.
>
> —NUMBERS 27:7

The chayil woman considers a field and buys it. She plants a vineyard.

> She considereth a field, and buyeth it: with the fruit of her hands she planteth a vineyard.
>
> —PROVERBS 31:16

The chayil woman engages in commerce.

> She is like the merchants' ships; she bringeth her food from afar.
>
> —PROVERBS 31:14

> She buys imported foods brought by ship from distant ports.
>
> —PROVERBS 31:14, TLB

FROM A SPIRIT OF POVERTY TO A SPIRIT OF CREATIVITY AND INNOVATION WITH SOPHIA RUFFIN

Sophia Ruffin participated in the Chayil Woman Challenge and allowed me to interview her about her testimony and how God has moved in various aspects of her life. I asked her to share her testimony about how she went from a typical nine-to-five job that she hated to an international ministry. She courageously stepped out and pursued all that God had for her life. She's written books. She's traveling the country. She's doing webinars and conferences. This all took courage. But there's also something she awakened to about wealth that I think will bless you. God wants to use chayil women to generate wealth. You can break out of a spirit of poverty, lack, and limitations and instead move in creativity, innovation, and wealth. Sophia shares how God did this for her:

> Yes, it did take a lot of courage to walk off that job. I was a social worker for thirteen years, and my highest pay as a social worker was thirty-eight thousand dollars a year. I was just going to work every day, going through the motions. I was speaking in tongues and praying. People thought I quit my job to pursue full-time ministry, but I actually didn't have anything but three oh-ye-faithful engagements that I went to every year when I quit my job. I didn't have any

63

books. So I wasn't stepping out because I had something; I stepped out on faith.

I kept saying, "I'm sick of this job. I'm tired of it."

At the time, it was winter, and you know, it's below zero in Chicago. I'm walking downtown crying. My tears froze to my face. When I got into the office, I looked at my ashy face and said to myself, "This is the last time I'm going to do this. I can't keep doing it." I knew God had more for me and that He didn't call me to just sit.

I was sick of the poverty demon in my bloodline. I wanted to do something different with my life. I had been faithful. I sowed what I had. I tithed.

One day a situation came where the supervisor came and did the right thing at the right time. I said, "All right. Enough is enough." I walked out on faith and said, "I just need ten days. If I get ten days, I'm going to produce a miracle."

I didn't know what was next for me, but I wrote my first book in those ten days. I used my last check as well as my vacation pay and invested in my book. And things just broke open.

Immediately when I left, I started doing my Periscopes and videos. I started being consistent and just hit this flow. My confidence began to build. And all of a sudden, there was a ripple effect. There were divine connections...that connecting to your life and ministry. Even more ripples began to happen.

I believe God will reward your courage. He rewards those who have guts. Chayil women have the guts to do whatever God is calling them to do. For me, it was scary. I was thinking, "What if something goes wrong?" But then I said, "Wait. I'm so focused on what could go wrong. What if it can go right?"

If I have God, if I have faith, and I step out on faith and have guts—I just do it—something can go right. I believe that. When I did, financially everything broke open for me. Financially I began to see God break that poverty spirit in me. I began to see myself in a place to be financially blessed. It came from stepping out and being courageous and not always looking at what can go wrong.

We, as a people, especially women, are worried and concerned about everything else. We look around, saying, "Man, this can go wrong. This can go wrong. This can go wrong." But we are people of faith. We pray. We have God. So why do we always put emphasis on what can go wrong? In my life I reversed that. I thought about what could go right. I thought about being a best-selling author. I told myself that I can write books. Doors can open for me. I can become creative. I can invest in myself. And that's what I did. Ever since then, it's been a wrap.

I have written five books and two e-books. No, I did not do well in school. One year in school I made straight Fs. I just remember saying, "My God! That's horrible!" I never ever thought until a few years ago that I would write a book.[4]

It is amazing what God has done in Sophia's life. She is hosting conferences all over the country. She mentors women of all ages and backgrounds through her Comeback Kid (CBK) Squad. She has a podcast. She's doing webinars. She's using her money wisely.

I know her testimony. I know where she came from. At one point she thought she would end up in the WNBA but didn't make it. That in itself can be devastating. The enemy came in and tried to make her feel like a failure, that she could never come back. But then she got delivered, got saved, and began to believe God.

Sophia is faithful in ministry, and after leaving her job and being obedient to share her testimony, the Lord elevated and exalted her in due season. The spirit of poverty has been broken off her life. She is walking in favor, blessing, and abundance. This is the life of a chayil woman.

THE CHAYIL WOMAN AND WEALTH WITH MICHELLE McCLAIN-WALTERS

Chayil women are women of wealth. Deuteronomy 8:18 says, "God will give you the power to get wealth." The word *power* means "strength (of angels)" or a "capacity" to get chayil.[5] It represents the "power (of God)."[6] So God is saying that He will give you the capacity to get wealth. For women who carry the chayil anointing, the wealth and riches He's going to give to us will help break the power of systemic poverty that has been in the earth.

When you look at the statistics, people who are most affected by poverty are women and children. I believe that, as chayil women, God is going to show us how to be humanitarians. He is going to show us how to effectively get wealth. He doesn't want us squandering our money. God is going to give [us] a new mind-set as it relates to money.

As we learn that God will give us the power to get wealth, how do we get it? We have to learn about investments, franchises, and more. God is going to give us a capacity. He is going to enlarge us. We will think big. The devil has caused women to think that we don't have any power, and we don't have any might, but the devil is a liar. God is breaking that spirit off of you, and you are going to understand that God is giving you the power to get wealth. He is going to give you creativity.

With chayil women, we have the wisdom of God. The spirit of wisdom comes with an ability to create things. God will show you.

I am praying for the spirit of wisdom and revelation to rest upon you. There are things in the spirit that are waiting to exist. Creativity is how those things come down out of the spirit realm into the earth. I am believing that God is giving chayil women power to get wealth to establish His covenant.[7]

Chapter 4

A WOMAN of WORSHIP,
PRAYER, and FAITH

PAMELA HARDY HAS been such a blessing to my life in ministry. She has brought her dance teams to every Asaph Gathering. What she is doing in ministry in the Dallas area and around the world is phenomenal. The impact she's having on so many people amazes me.

Pamela has been in ministry for a number of years, raising up dance, prophetic, and apostolic teams. She does it all. She even has written three books: *Dance: The Higher Call, Unlocking Your Prophetic Destiny,* and *Far Above Rubies: The Power of Christ's Virtue in You.*[1]

When I found out that she also had been teaching about chayil, I knew I wanted to have her join me on my Facebook Live broadcast. When she came on, I asked her to talk about her revelation of chayil and what God has given her in this particular area concerning women. Here's how our conversation went:

PH: I learned about this revelation of chayil a few years ago. The root word of *chayil*, *chuwl*, means to turn in a circular manner as in dancing.[2] So you can imagine how excited I was when I found out that the root word is *chuwl* [pronounced "cool"], which is connected to dance and to worship. I started reading and studying because worship is the foundation of everything that we do.

Going back to the beginning just for a second, I should tell you that I got saved dancing on Broadway. Yes, I did. I went to New York City. When I was there, *Dreamgirls* was on Broadway. They had a Bible study, the Bible study turned into a church, and the church was pastored by a woman. She's a chayil woman. Through that experience, I started to learn that women can be strong. Women can have a voice. God has a plan for women.

So, back to the present. When I found out about chayil women, the Lord really impressed upon my heart to start a company of chayil women—a global initiative. I have chapters in British Virgin Islands. I just got back from Bolivia and St. Thomas. God is moving, and women are saying, "Yes, that's me! I know I'm powerful. I know I'm a force." We even have shirts that say "Chayil Force." We are raising up ladies all over the world, and it's just exciting what God is doing.[3]

Me: We had a phenomenal gathering with you in Orlando and Dallas with the Asaph Gatherings. We're coming together again in the months to come. It's amazing how you gather and raise up hundreds of people. You've imparted. You've trained. You've raised up some powerful women of God—and this word *chayil* means strength, strong, and warrior.

One of the amazing things about your prophetic dance ministry is that every time I start prophesying, you seem to have a banner with the prophetic word on it. You have all these banners, and you always have a banner with the exact words that I'm prophesying because you actually pray before you come to the conference and ask God what banners [to use].

Another thing is that you're really into beauty, beautiful garments and the beauty of God. Chayil represents the beauty and glory of God.

You shared your testimony about how you were saved when you went to Broadway to be a dancer. Tell us about your journey and about how you grew in the things of God. You're very unusual having the prophetic, apostolic, and deliverance. You're not ordinary. You've learned a lot over the years. Tell me some of the people who have affected your life and influenced you to walk in the strength and the power you operate in now.

PH: After I got saved dancing on Broadway, I actually went and taught at Illinois State University. While I was teaching, God began to open doors. Apostle John, I used to have a prison ministry, and we were going to one prison in the morning, one prison in the afternoon, and another in the evening. I loved prison ministry, and I loved women's ministry. So the Lord said, "OK, it's time to leave that and focus on what I've called you to do in the area of worship."

Now He's brought it back full circle to the women's ministry. But I'm going to tell you what I tell everybody. My favorite scripture is Proverbs 8:34–35. It says, "Blessed is the man that heareth me, watching daily at my gates, waiting at the posts of my doors. For whoso findeth me findeth life, and shall obtain favour of the LORD."

I think that's what did it. I would just worship every day. When I got saved, my pastor said that the way you get delivered, stay delivered, walk into your destiny, stay free, do the things God wants you to do, is by getting to know Him and building that relationship. It was all just Holy Spirit.

I would be in my room worshipping, and my phone would ring. I would get an email. It would be a call to Holland. I don't know anybody in Holland. It would be a call to come to South Africa, Bolivia, or Cuba. This is all just from my being in that place before the Lord.

God is well able to do everything that He purposed for our lives if we'll just stay in that place with Him.

WORSHIP AS THE KEY TO WALKING IN CHAYIL

As Pamela and I continued our conversation, I wanted to dive deeper into her dancing and praise ministry and how important worship is to being a strong woman of God.

Me: You love dancing. You love worshipping God. I've seen you do it with your teams. I've seen you at our Asaph Gatherings, where we worship for hours to new songs. There's dancing and celebration. I believe that there is a grace and an anointing that comes on a person's life when they learn how to worship.

The Bible says that Miriam led the women in the timbrel and the dance when they came out of the Red Sea (Exod. 15:20). Then Psalm 48:11 says, "Let mount Zion rejoice, let the daughters of Judah be glad, because of thy judgments." This verse emphasizes the daughters, and it is connected to Zion and the kingdom. Tell us your revelation of why you feel dancing is so important to being a strong woman of God. God has given you a revelation about praise and worship but especially the dance ministry.[4]

PH: The thing is this: Miriam led all the women in the dance. Those were dances of victory, dances of rejoicing. The reason is because she was the closest female relative to Moses. It was a custom for the closest female relative to meet and greet the returning victor after there was a battle. Our returning victor is Jesus. Hallelujah! The closer His return gets, the more you're going to see an increase in dancing because we as His betrothed—we, the church—are His closest female relatives, and we're going to usher Him back with dancing and rejoicing and shouting.

Every culture actually has dances that are indigenous to their particular culture. In our culture it's love, joy, peace, long-suffering, gentleness, and goodness. All those have an expression of movement in the kingdom. When we dance, the Lord says He's given us the authority in our feet. Every piece of ground that the soles of our feet tread upon is given to us. The Word says that we tread upon serpents and scorpions. Our feet represent authority, so our dance is powerful. Our dance is full of strength. Our dance relates to victory. There's even a dance of intercession sometimes that God will bring upon you to birth you into new things.

Dance can take many different forms. Sometimes dance is prophetic. Sometimes we're receiving from heaven and releasing it to the earth. Sometimes we're just having congregational dance to rejoice in the goodness of the Lord and of who He is. He says to let them praise His name in the dance. "Them" means everybody. We have permission to worship Him in the dance.

I believe everybody is called to worship the Lord in the dance because there's such an expression about dance that words can't always say. If people would just be free and step into that place of expression and worship with the Lord, they will see that there's nothing that brings that kind of power.

Dancing to Release the Bonds of the Chayil Woman

Dancing represents liberty, and for years women have not been free in the church. They were told they couldn't preach, teach, or do anything but fry chicken in the kitchen. Maybe they could be ushers. Some churches today tell women they can't minister, they can't be called, and they can't move in certain things because they're women. God wants to set women free. You cannot be a chayil woman if you're not free and you don't have liberty. The enemy loves to bind women with tradition, religion, cultural bondages, control, manipulation, and domination by men in society. But God is setting women free. The Bible says, "Where the Spirit of the Lord is, there is liberty" (2 Cor. 3:17), and there is liberty in worship and dance.

In the closing minutes of our interview, Pamela gave the following parting words. I know you will be strengthened by her impartation:

> In Psalm 110:3 it says [in essence] that this is the day of His chayil power. We're living in the day of God's chayil power. As you read this right now, I pray that the chayil anointing that God has for you that's already resident on the inside of you—that innate ability—will rise up. He said that He called those who are able. "Able" is the word *chayil*. He put able men in position to be rulers.
>
> I pray that the chayil anointing that's already in you will rise up, and you will have no more fear. I pray that you will step into the force of that chayil anointing and unlock the wealth, unlock your potential, unlock strength, and

unlock the glory. I pray that you would see God in a new way, that His favor may be unlocked over your life. Let the chayil anointing come and be released over your life, and let it unlock those things in you that need to be restored. Let it unlock your ability. Let it unlock power. Let it unlock your peace. It will unlock wealth that you need for your family. It will unlock your dreams and your visions.

I'm hearing that some of you have been having torment in the night season, but God will give you peace in your sleep. You will sleep like you've never slept before, in Jesus' name.

I hear for some of you there's a fear. You've been wanting to step into it. God says to just embrace this chayil anointing. Embrace the force of this and step into this. You're going to see doors open for you like never before.

I see that vision is going to be open for some of you, in Jesus' name. I see that your ears will be opened. You will hear things that you never heard before.

I'm hearing God say, "This is the season to spend time with Me." God is saying, "Come into My presence. Let Me pour into you those things that I want you to have. Take the blessing I have for you. Do not take on the identity other people would want to put upon you. Don't take any identity that you have for yourself." God says, "Let Me put My identity in you and upon you. And I'm going to send you forth in so much power that even you won't recognize yourself." Hallelujah! God says, "I have things for you. They're in there. But you have been even afraid to see them. You've been even afraid to recognize them. You've been even afraid to say out of your mouth, 'Lord, this is what I see. This is what I'm believing You for.'" We break that now in the name of Jesus.

Those of you who have been wanting to step into the areas of ministry, this is your time. This is your season. This is not the season to back up. This is the season to grab ahold of the strength, power, and force of the chayil anointing and go forward in the power of your God. For He is great in the midst of you.[5]

My interview with Pamela Hardy confirmed what the Lord had been revealing to me about chayil women.

Chayil women love God's presence.

They love giving to the house of the Lord. They love giving God glory. They flourish in the house of the Lord. Chayil women are able to come into God's courts and get their prayer requests answered by the King.

Chayil women are worshippers.

They love strong praise and worship. They love the glory realm. Chayil is mentioned twice in Isaiah 60. Isaiah 60 is a command to rise and shine, for the glory of the Lord is risen upon you.

Chayil women are glory carriers.

> Let mount Zion rejoice, let the daughters of Judah be glad, because of thy judgments.
>
> —PSALM 48:11

Chayil women love Zion.

They have Zion hearts. The daughters of Judah are filled with joy and gladness. The joy of the Lord is the chayil woman's strength.

> And God said unto Abraham, As for Sarai thy wife, thou shalt not call her name Sarai, but Sarah shall her name be. And I will bless her, and give thee a son also of her: yea, I will bless her, and she shall be a mother of nations; kings of people shall be of her.
>
> —GENESIS 17:15–16

Chayil women are women of great faith.

Sarai was a chayil woman. She became a mother of nations. She is also mentioned in the "hall of faith" (Hebrews 11) because she received strength to conceive through faith.

I admire women of great faith. Jesus recognized women of great faith as well.

> Then Jesus answered and said unto her, O woman, great is thy faith: be it unto thee even as thou wilt. And her daughter was made whole from that very hour.
>
> —MATTHEW 15:28

A HEART TO PRAY WITH VALORA SHAW-COLE

The chayil woman is strong in prayer. I introduced you to Valora Shaw-Cole in chapter 1, but I wanted to include her insights in this chapter about prayer. She has a very strong intercessory prayer ministry. She prays strong. I believe her strong prayer life has carried her to the level she is at now. I asked her to share with me how all of that developed for her and to encourage women in how they too can develop their prayer lives and become strong chayil women of prayer. This is what she said:

> I've always had a heart to pray, but because I was so shy as a child, I would not open my mouth to verbally pray. I would just write God letters. I would write Him and tell Him about the things that were on my heart. God is so amazing. He began to answer those prayers.
>
> I had such a hunger. I used to ask God, "Please teach me how to pray."

You know, even in church I would hear people pray, and I just wanted that relationship with God. I would sit in my room—I was an only child—and just meditate on God. I just wanted to know who He was. I had such a hunger for prayer.

I began to study various books on prayer. I read Charles Capps' books. I read Norvel Hayes. Prayer really became alive in me. God began to teach me how to pray the Word, to pray the solution and not the problem. Even in my denominational church that I grew up in I would hear people pray the problem. They would say, "God, please help me. Please heal me if it's Your will." I always felt that something was not right in what I was hearing.

God began to open my eyes to understand how to pray effectively, and I began to see results. It turned out, then, that I wanted everybody to understand how to pray effectively. I bought hundreds of books, and I would just give them away to people because I wanted them to come into the knowledge of truth. It is the truth that makes us free, and the level of truth you receive determines the level of freedom you walk in.

So, with my husband—which is an amazing part of my life because he really pushed me—I remember the first book that we wrote together,

Plug Into the Power of Prayer and Prophetic Intercession.[6] Initially it was just something we wanted to do for our local church, but the interest and hunger in our church community began to grow. I began to do training, not just in my local church but in different places as well.

My husband said, "Valora, there's something else inside you concerning prayer."

I said, "Well, I feel that too, but I'm not exactly sure what I need to call it. What title should it be?" Many of times I have relied on my husband to help me.

He would say, "Just think about it. I'll come back to you a little later."

He really tried to do everything he could to push me and to cultivate that next level inside of me. So one day he came back to me and said, "I really believe it has something to do with bold and something to do with fearless."

Receiving his input, I took time to fast and pray and seek God, and He showed me that I should call it "The Bold Prayer Warrior" and "The Fearless Intercessor." That revelation really blew my mind. I researched it, but I couldn't find it anywhere, so I knew it came directly from God. It was original. Through ministering in this vein, I really tackled that enemy called fear, because, as I said, fear had paralyzed me for so many years. It had silenced me.

A few years ago I did a conference called I Am Fearless. It was really amazing. Out of that came a thirty-one-day journal: *I Am Fearless Journal.* [7] I modeled the journal after this time frame because researchers say it takes thirty-one days to break a habit and start something new. I wanted women to come together even during that conference and face their fears. I even did a Fearless Challenge, where I challenged women to submit a two- or three-minute video identifying one particular event or situation that occurred in their lives that moved them from being fearful to being fearless. The response was amazing. Women who had been in sex trafficking for over ten years submitted videos. They shared how one day they decided that they were going to rise up and tell someone.

It's just been an amazing process. Prayer is my heart. It's my passion for everyone to understand the power of prayer, their position in prayer, and what God wants to do in prayer. I want them to know it's about more than just telling God what they want and need. I want them to know that God also wants to reveal His heart to us through prayer so that we understand who we are in Him.[8]

What Valora's life and ministry reveal is that women are called to war against the powers of hell spiritually. Women make tremendous prayer warriors, tremendous intercessors. Chayil women are strong women of prayer, intercession, and spiritual warfare.

The prayers and intercession of a chayil woman bring deliverance and enlargement. Anna was a chayil woman of prayer. She was a prophetess who served God with fasting and prayer day and night.

> And there was one Anna, a prophetess, the daughter of Phanuel, of the tribe of Aser: she was of a great age, and had lived with an husband seven years from her virginity; and she was a widow of about fourscore and four years, which departed not from the temple, but served God with fastings and prayers night and day.
>
> —LUKE 2:36–37

Anna's prayers helped pave the way for the Messiah to come. Chayil women serve God. In this case Anna served in the temple through prayer and fasting.

In closing the broadcast, Valora recited a declaration for women to be released and to become fearless and bold, especially in the area of prayer. I encourage you to speak it aloud even now as you read it here:

> I am strong-willed. I have a heart of gold. I am beautiful, both inside and out. I am able to push

through storms of a shattered heart, broken spirit, and a tattered body. I emerge from the storm twice as graceful and independent. I am a truly gifted woman with a gorgeous soul. This is who I am. I am courageous. I am bold. I am fearless. I am determined.[9]

Chapter 5

A WOMAN of RARE and NOBLE CHARACTER

T HE CHAYIL WOMAN is rare. Who can find her? Men, you must find her. For her price is far above rubies (Prov. 31:10). Her type and characteristics are not present in every woman. She's like a ruby. She's rare. She's valuable. She's not easy to find. Sometimes she's a diamond in the rough. You have to look beyond what's around and discover this virtuous chayil woman because she's the one who has strength, power, might, business, efficiency, and wealth. She's able to handle a business. She's a strong woman. She's not just any kind of woman. She's not meant to be a sex object. Some men don't look for a virtuous woman. They want a loose woman until they're ready to get married; then they want a virtuous woman.

When some men go out to the clubs, they are not looking for virtuous women. They are looking for unvirtuous women. But then when a man is looking for a virtuous woman, he goes to church, saying, "I'm believing God for a good wife."

But, woman of God, if you are single, even as this happens, you must use discernment. Some men are saved only from the waist up. They are not saved from the waist down.

A chayil woman is worthy of a man who is fully saved from the top of his head to the soles of his feet. And a chayil woman will not compromise in this area. She is strong enough to say no to something or someone who is not God's best for her. She is strong enough to live holy and clean. She is strong enough to overcome temptation. She is strong enough to live a fully saved life.

Woman of God, I know it takes strength to be a saved woman today because there are more women in the church than men. It takes strength to be a saved woman today because the enemy will try to tell you that you're never going to get married unless you compromise. He'll try to tempt you, saying, "Go out there and get one, marry him, and bring him to church and get him saved."

It takes strength and might to live holy. It takes might to go home alone and fight against demons of loneliness. And it's not that men aren't interested. You are attractive, you have your life together, and men see this in you and try to approach. But you say no.

The chayil woman is noble, poised, kind, and generous; guards her tongue; keeps good company; is a good friend; and exhibits well all the fruit of the Spirit. She honors and respects her husband. She speaks the truth in love. She teaches her children to walk in the ways of the Lord. She conducts business with strong intellect, authority, and wisdom. Who can find a woman like this? She is rare and hard to find.

THE CHAYIL WOMAN IS ROYAL, NOBLE, AND HONORABLE

Chayil women are kings' daughters. Kings' daughters are honorable women.

> Kings' daughters were among thy honourable women: upon thy right hand did stand the queen in gold of Ophir.
>
> —PSALM 45:9

In Scripture kings would marry other kings' daughters. This is royalty. This is majesty. These daughters are used to the royal courts. They are noblewomen. Chayil women live and minister in the King's courts. Esther came into the court of the king, and he extended the golden scepter to her.

Chayil women love the courts of God and are planted there.

> Those that be planted in the house of the LORD shall flourish in the courts of our God.
>
> —PSALM 92:13

> Give unto the LORD the glory due unto his name: bring an offering, and come into his courts.
>
> —PSALM 96:8

My soul longeth, yea, even fainteth for the courts
of the LORD: my heart and my flesh crieth out
for the living God.

—PSALM 84:2

THE CHAYIL WOMAN IS VALUABLE

The chayil woman is a woman of strength and honor. She is
more valuable than precious stones.

Who can find a virtuous woman? for her price is
far above rubies.

—PROVERBS 31:10

Strength and honour are her clothing; and she
shall rejoice in time to come.

—PROVERBS 31:25

We met Lady Wisdom in the opening chapters
of the Book of Proverbs. We also find her in the
closing verses of that same book. Proverbs 31:10
asks, "A capable wife who can find? She is far
more precious than jewels" (NRSV). Has Lady
Wisdom been demoted to merely a "capable
wife"? Unfortunately, most translations from
Hebrew into English obscure the implications
of the original text. The word translated as
"capable" is the Hebrew word *chayil*, which, as
we have seen, means mighty, strong, valiant, and

is used in the Old Testament 242 times, usually to describe soldiers or armies. In 2 Samuel 23 we learn that David's "mighty men" were chayil for their courage and strength. Here in Proverbs 31:10 it should read, "A valiant woman who can find? She is far more precious than jewels."[1]

She openeth her mouth with wisdom; and in her tongue is the law of kindness.

—PROVERBS 31:26

THE CHAYIL WOMAN—A DISTINCT IDENTITY WITH MICHELLE MCCLAIN-WALTERS

I started with Apostle John's ministry when I was twenty-four years old. I've been there for twenty-eight years. It's been a process. What does the chayil grace look like on me? It looks different.

One of the things God is doing is giving us all a distinct identity, and it includes a grace for action. He is saying that the chayil woman is not inactive and fearful, but she is a woman of courage and boldness. She is a woman who moves forward in power and glory.

What God has done in my life as a prophet is that many times He has called me to be a fore-runner. I believe there have been times when

God has positioned my life—things that I've walked through—like that of a forerunner.

I was so excited to learn that Apostle John had written this book. There is such a call on his life that when he does something like this, it is like a clarion call to those with an ear in the body of Christ. So as you read this book, it should be activating something on the inside of you.

The Bible tells us in Psalm 68:11, "The Lord gave the word..." He gave a command. This book is like a command where God is saying, "The trumpet is sounding. This is a set time, women. I don't want you to miss your timing. I don't want you to miss your season of visitation."

This is the set time that God is favoring Zion. The set time means the opportune time. Women and men, this is a time when God is raising us up in team ministry. I believe we are getting ready to go into a season where men are not going to be afraid to pour into strong women and strong women are not going to be afraid to receive from strong men.

Many of the things the Lord has done in my life—I tell you, fifty-four nations later—are because I submitted to a chayil man. Apostle John Eckhardt has poured into my life. There were even times when he made room on his platform for me. These are the days when God is bringing unity between male and female. We are going to celebrate our differences. This chayil movement with women is not going to be like a feminist movement that says, "Man, I don't need you. I can do anything you can do."

The devil is a liar. We are not every woman, and it is not all in us. What God is going to show is, yes, you are a woman. Yes, you can move together with men and remain in your femininity. God is calling chayil women to embrace their femininity.

In the spirit, I saw a company of women coming together. God said, "Great is the power of women." He is going to give us power. I saw an army of women marching together in unity, but we had our distinction. We were feminine; we were not like men, but we honored men.

Chayil women understand that one can chase a thousand and two can put ten thousand to flight. Men and women can do more together than we can apart. I believe God is breaking off the spirit of gender prejudice. As chayil women, we're understanding who we are. No longer will we be trapped by traditions. We are distinct, and this is our strength.[2]

Chapter 6

A WOMAN of POWER and INFLUENCE

THE CHAYIL WOMAN is a woman of power, influence, wealth, strength, ability, wisdom, virtue, faith, prayer, prophecy, and might. She knows how to pray. She knows how to prophesy. She knows how to decree. She knows how to bind the devil. She knows how to cast out devils. She knows how to worship. She knows how to praise God. She knows how to study the Word. She has authority and influence in her home and in the marketplace. She speaks with wisdom, and those who listen to her counsel are blessed.

Women were never created by God to be weak. They were created with man to exercise dominion. Women were never created to be under man's feet but by his side. Women are corulers with men.

Jesus came to set women free from the traditions of culture and bring them into their rightful place of power and strength. The one word *chayil* is loaded with power and revelation. Chayil women are rising up in the church and in society. Let chayil women arise and walk in the power and might of God.

In this chapter I catalog and give examples of biblical women who exhibited the chayil characteristics of power, authority, and influence in various spheres of culture and society. I also will introduce you to another of my spiritual daughters who walks in power and influence but didn't start there until she started to walk in her anointing.

REBEKAH, A CHAYIL WOMAN OF POWER, AUTHORITY, AND INFLUENCE

Rebekah was called a mother of thousands of millions. In other words, she would be a mother of billions. This is chayil. This is power and influence.

> And they blessed Rebekah, and said unto her, Thou art our sister, be thou the mother of thousands of millions, and let thy seed possess the gate of those which hate them.
> —GENESIS 24:60

Rebekah's seed (Jesus) would possess the gate of His enemies. This is dominion. This is power and authority. This is what a chayil woman will birth and bring forth. The blessing of Rebekah speaks to these characteristics of chayil women.

DEBORAH, A CHAYIL MOTHER BOTH
NATURALLY AND SPIRITUALLY

Deborah was a mother in Israel.

> The inhabitants of the villages ceased, they
> ceased in Israel, until that I Deborah arose, that
> I arose a mother in Israel.
>
> —JUDGES 5:7

Mothers birth, nurture, care for, and protect. Deborah operated in these strengths for an entire nation.

Michelle McClain-Walters wrote a book called *The Deborah Anointing*,[1] and when she spoke on this topic during the Chayil Woman Challenge, she said this:

> It wasn't Deborah's prophetic grace that caused
> her to arise, even though it did help her. It was
> not her ability as a judge, and it wasn't even the
> warrior in her. It was the mother in Deborah
> that caused her to arise on behalf of her nation.
>
> God is raising up strong chayil women who
> understand that they are mothers and have been
> called to birth life. Chayil women are givers of
> life. God is releasing strong apostolic mothers
> because it takes mothers and fathers to raise up
> sons and daughters.
>
> The Lord showed me this: He said, "Michelle,
> the greatest tragedy in the earth is not abortion.

The tragedy is that the devil has taken the mother's heart out of women." So as chayil women we need to rise up and be the natural and spiritual mothers God has called us to be.

We need to disciple the next generation of women. We need to teach them to love who they are. We can teach them, "No, you don't want to abort your child. You want to raise your child." We need to embrace them and show them how to embrace their femininity. We need to let them know that they don't have to be like a man or move like a man to be established and favored. Being fully who God called them to be is enough.

These are the days [when] as chayil women we understand the power of discipleship. We understand the power to reproduce after our own kind.

So you hear this clarion call. You are reading this book, and you are wondering, "What do I do with this anointing?" Disciple. Disciple that young woman who is sitting right next to you.

When you begin to reproduce after your own kind, the kingdom of God is advanced. Don't be afraid to pour your life into the next generation. We cannot be selfish. We have to let the mother's heart come inside of us. I have gotten more things done in the realm of the spirit as a mother and a daughter. You must understand who you are, and do not despise what God has placed on the inside of you. These are the days when God is raising us up to counsel, to train.

Deborah was able to counsel as she sat under the juniper tree. She was in a place where she was touchable.

As chayil women, we have the ability to reproduce and to pour our lives into the next generation as well as our own children.[2]

Miriam, a Chayil Woman, an Apostolic Woman

Chayil women can be sent. Miriam was a prophetess, but she was also apostolic. She was sent with Moses and Aaron to deliver Israel.

> And Miriam the prophetess, the sister of Aaron, took a timbrel in her hand; and all the women went out after her with timbrels and with dances.
> —Exodus 15:20

> For I brought thee up out of the land of Egypt, and redeemed thee out of the house of servants; and I sent before thee Moses, Aaron, and Miriam.
> —Micah 6:4

God does call and send women. Moses, Aaron, and Miriam represent an apostolic team. Chayil women are sent women.

THE WOMAN OF SHUNEM, A CHAYIL WOMAN OF GREATNESS

Elisha met a prominent, influential, and wealthy noble-woman. Chayil women are women of wealth. They are prosperous women.

> And it fell on a day, that Elisha passed to Shunem, where was a great woman; and she constrained him to eat bread. And so it was, that as oft as he passed by, he turned in thither to eat bread.
>
> —2 KINGS 4:8

> One day Elisha went on to Shunem, where a rich and influential woman lived, who insisted on his eating a meal. Afterward, whenever he passed by, he stopped there for a meal.
>
> —2 KINGS 4:8, AMPC

This woman of Shunem was a chayil woman who blessed and supported the ministry of Elisha. Chayil women are a great blessing to the ministry. Every church needs chayil women who support the ministry in prayer and finance. Chayil women have power to get wealth (Deut. 8:18), and their wealth supports ministries, breaks the spirit of poverty, and expands the kingdom.

ESTHER, A CHAYIL WOMAN OF FAVOR

Esther is an example of a chayil woman of favor. She went from obscurity to becoming a queen.

> And it was so, when the king saw Esther the queen standing in the court, that she obtained favour in his sight: and the king held out to Esther the golden sceptre that was in his hand. So Esther drew near, and touched the top of the sceptre.
>
> —ESTHER 5:2

Esther's favor and influence delivered the nation from the plot of Haman. Esther also represents intercession.

CHAYIL WOMEN USE THEIR WEALTH AND INFLUENCE TO BREAK BARRIERS

According to *The Economist*, "By 2020 [women] are expected to hold $72 trillion, 32 percent of the total. And most of the private wealth that changes hands in the coming decades is likely to go to women."[3]

Women are becoming wealthier as barriers are broken and new levels are achieved. Women are now handling more wealth than at any other time in history. This brings them into greater levels of influence and power. Being chayil, their wisdom also brings wealth and honor into their lives. The wealth, power, influence, and wisdom of chayil women are breaking the cycles of poverty that have afflicted many families for generations.

BATTLING THE SPIRIT OF FEAR AND INTIMIDATION WITH YOLANDA STITH

During my Facebook Live Chayil Woman Challenge in June 2018 I interviewed one of Apostle Matthew Stevenson's spiritual daughters, Apostle Yolanda Stith. Apostle Stevenson is one of my spiritual sons who is doing great work out of his home base, All Nations Worship Assembly in Chicago, and its seven other campuses, located around the United States and Canada. He raised up Yolanda, and she is now leading All Nations Worship Assembly in Baltimore, Maryland. She is a great preacher. She is strong in prayer and intercession. She is apostolic, is prophetic, and moves in the gifts of God. I invited her on the broadcast to share her journey because people may see her preaching, praying, and prophesying and not understand where she came from. Everyone has a journey. No one really starts off strong and powerful. We have to grow into it.

Initially Yolanda struggled with crippling fear. She is not alone. I have found that many powerful, strong, and influential women of God have had to overcome the spirit of fear and intimidation even as they accepted the call of God on their lives. I believe her testimony will speak to many women who need victory over fear and bondages placed on them by society and male-dominated mind-sets. She says:

I was saved twenty-two years ago when a friend invited me to a very small church. A prophet was ministering there. I sat on the very back row because I was skeptical. The woman began to preach, and she preached with such power and began to call on the name of Jesus. All of a sudden this yell came out of me, where demons were leaving me, but simultaneously I was filled with the Holy Ghost. My journey starts there.

From that point I was on fire, witnessing and evangelizing, but I was still going to a Baptist church. I finally found a place that was prophetic, and I started with this woman who taught me the things of the Spirit and about prayer.

My prayer ministry started with just me and Jesus. I had keys to the church, so I would go there a few days a week at five o'clock. I would pray for hours without any recognition from my pastor. No one else was there. I would just pray because I love the presence of God, and I began to understand what the power of prayer could do. So for years I just prayed because I love prayer. I walked with God because I am in love with Jesus.

I was a very tormented young girl. I was tormented by devils. I was bound by fear and did not believe God could do anything with my life.

Then all of a sudden God saved me, delivered me, and set me free.

When I started serving Him, I knew that without Him I would be nothing. The kingdom of darkness had an assignment for my life to kill and destroy me. I had two nervous break-downs—one at fifteen and one at nineteen years old—because my life was just so traumatic. But God spared my mind, gave me a purpose to live, and I am walking out this journey today.[4]

I believe, based on Psalm 68:11, that God is raising up a strong group of women who preach and declare. I had Yolanda share more about how she became the strong preacher that she is. Here's what she said:

I took a preaching class. Then I accepted my first assignment to preach. I preached a message called "You Can't Run From God." It was really my own story. I had a pastor who was very com-mitted to making sure I fulfilled the plan of God from the very beginning. I began to develop this message, but fear gripped me in such a way that when I stood up, my knees began to buckle. I lit-erally lost all strength in my body. It took every-thing within me to stand and preach my first sermon.

For me, it didn't get easier. It got harder because I was tormented with thoughts of

"What's going to happen if you mess up?" "What about this?" "What about that?" So for me, as a woman, I always would find the reason why I wasn't qualified or the reason why people would not want to hear me. I had to overcome fear in order to do what I am doing today.

I would rehearse scriptures and declare them over myself. I would say, "God has not given me the spirit of fear, but of power, love, and a sound mind." I would say these verses as I walked up to the pulpit to preach.

I feel as if fear is a guardian spirit. It's the guardian of destiny. It stands at the door of destiny. So whenever fear is present, I feel as if there's something on the other side. For me, that's been my testimony. Whenever I've been extremely afraid of something, I have seen that on the other side of the fear is something God wants to get to me. So I would get up, and when I would mount that pulpit and start to preach, the power of God would fill the room. People would get saved and delivered, and demons would manifest—all very early on in ministry for me. I had a total reliance on the Holy Spirit because I knew without Him I would fall flat on my face. I would crumble.

So even today I try to place total reliance on Him when I'm approaching any assignment because I know that at any moment if I ever gave way to that spirit again, it would overtake me. But God has brought me through so many deliverances.

I don't know that many people know this, but my mom is brain damaged. She has been brain damaged since I was two years old. I think that a lot of that fear came from an orphan heart. God taught me who He is as my Father, and that helped me walk as the woman of God I am today.[5]

Journey to becoming a female apostle

I was labeled very early on as a prophet. Inwardly I struggled with it, but because I was very prophetic and that's what my former leaders told me, I accepted it.

It wasn't until I met Dr. Matthew Stevenson that all that changed. He helped me put a language to who I was called to be, and it made so much sense. With such grace and such boldness, I entered into it, though I didn't embrace it at the beginning. When Apostle Stevenson sent me a message saying, "I want to ordain you as an apostle; I know it is your call," I agreed with him, but I was very afraid of what people would think about my being a woman apostle. But having Apostle Stevenson in my life, and through the coaching of God, I was able to embrace it. I knew that I would be disrespecting the Holy Spirit to deny and reject who He had called me to be. To keep myself from being in error with God, I embraced my call, and I gladly walked that out.

I know that I am an equipper. I love to see the body of Christ equipped. Journeying into the apostolic, I embrace the fact that I am an equipper. I love to build people. I love to build the body of Christ. I love to see the kingdom of God manifest here on earth now.[6]

Chayil woman, it's time to be released!

I believe it's time for women to be delivered, set free, and released into their call. I think that this is a time when there is a thrust, an opening for women. God is causing women to rise up all over the earth and take their rightful place. We've been oppressed, we've been bound, and we've been in bondage—and not just to spirits but also to men who don't want to see us come forth. But I am thankful for men who create spaces for women.

I want to encourage every woman and say that it is time for you to be released and set free from fear. It is time for you to be set free to walk in your calling or whatever it is that God has set for you to do. It's time for you to rise up and take your place.

Don't you know that when you are in your place, the kingdom of God will manifest quicker, it will come to earth, and God can do anything that He wants to do? You are that conduit of power. You are that woman God wants to come forth. It's time for you to be aggressive, violent, and bold about the place that God has set for you.

God is doing with women today what He did with Anna when He brought Jesus into the earth through her prayers. There are anointings such as Anna's, Deborah's, and those of other women in the Bible. It's time for you to rise up in those anointings and take your rightful place.

God wants to do with women what we've not been allowed to do for centuries. It's time for you to prophesy. It's time for you to cast out devils. It's time for you to gain the victory. You've been bound to fear too long.

I've ministered to so many women who say that they have been bound to fear and they are afraid to step out and preach. They are afraid to pray. They've asked me questions such as "What if I fail?" I ask them the question "What if you don't fail?"

Woman of God, it is time for you to overcome the fear of failure and step out.[7]

Chapter 7

PRAYERS and DECLARATIONS
for the CHAYIL WOMAN

WOMAN OF GOD, I know it takes strength to be holy and uncompromising. I know it takes strength to remain focused on the call of God on your life despite this world's distractions. I know that being rare isn't easy, that standing out, being set apart, and being unique can mean that most of the time you are going at it alone—just you and God. Who can find a woman like you? Who can keep up with your strength and power? Who can keep up with your efficiency? Who can keep up with the glory of God that shines through every area of your life? You are rare and highly valued by God.

I pray that you have been encouraged by the message in this book, that you have come to accept who you are in God, and that you will be bold in living out your virtue, strength, wealth, efficiency, and ability. Do not hide. Do not make yourself smaller for any man, woman, or child. Be all that God has created you to be. I pray now that this chayil anointing be activated in your life and that you find strength in the prayers and declarations I've included in this chapter.

DECLARATIONS THAT ACTIVATE
THE CHAYIL ANOINTING

Lord, let the chayil of God be in my life—virtue, power, strength, ability, business, efficiency, and might. Let it all be released into my life.

Thank You, Lord, for Your chayil—Your might, Your power, and Your strength—in my life. I will walk in it all the days of my life.

I believe in the spirit of might. I receive the spirit of might and the spirit of power into my life. I will not be weak. I will be strong. I will have the might of God in my life, in the name of Jesus.

Thank You, Lord, for the spirit of might being strongly upon me.

I believe it. I confess it. I declare it. I am a chayil believer.

I am a virtuous woman. I am a chayil woman. I am businesslike. I am efficient. I am strong. I have strength. I have wisdom. I have power. I have ability. I am not a weak woman. I am a chayil woman.

I will not draw back. I will not hide. I will let my virtue, power, and strength come forth.

God, You created me to be a chayil woman. Today, I take a step of faith, and I step into this chayil anointing, this chayil dimension, this chayil power, this chayil strength, in the name of Jesus.

Let me excel in business. Let me be efficient.

I decree that wealth and riches shall be in my life because of chayil and because of virtue.

Thank You, Lord. I release my faith today to activate this chayil anointing in my life. I decree it today, in Jesus' name.

I declare that this word will change my life and my perspective. I will not be that same person I used to be.

I declare that my standards are changing, my destiny is changing, and my confession and vision are changing. What I am believing God for is changing. My mind is being renewed.

Even if I am successful and experiencing God's favor, there's more. There's a higher level. I reach for the higher level. I reach for the prize of my high calling of God in Christ Jesus.

I accept who God has called me to be. I will not apologize for who God made me. I will step out boldly and courageously. I push back and cancel out the lies of the enemy and declare, "Devil, you're a liar."

I will not be held back. I will not be bound up. I will not be beat down. I will not allow anyone to use me as a doormat.

I will not be on the bottom. I will not be last. I will be the head and not the tail. I will be above and not beneath.

I am blessed coming in and blessed going out. I will lend to many nations, and I will not borrow. I'll be blessed in the city and blessed in the fields. I will be prosperous.

A PRAYER TO RELEASE THE POWER
OF CHAYIL IN YOUR LIFE

Lord, I pray for chayil grace to come upon my life. Lord, I pray that I will rise up in wealth, in the prophetic, in worship, in prayer, and in strength. Lord, I pray that I will rise up in vision, that I will be a powerful woman of God, a powerful daughter of the King. I pray that I will operate in power, wisdom, strength, ability, and wealth.

Father, I thank You that You are challenging me to be strong in You and the power of Your might. May I be strengthened with might in my inner being. May the spirits of counsel and might be upon me, in the name of Jesus.

I break cultural and religious traditions that have held me back. I pray for a release of Your anointing and grace, that I may rise up to be the woman You've ordained me to be. I am a daughter of the King.

I thank You, Father, for doing new things in my life. Let there be miracles and breakthroughs in every sphere that I influence. Let my life be changed as I behold Your glory. Let revelation be full. Let insight and understanding come as I receive a revelation for who I am as the chayil woman—a powerful woman, a woman of valor and strength, a valiant woman, and a woman of wealth. Let my faith go to another level, Lord, for whom You have called me to be. Break any limitation off of my life. I pray, and I bless You. In Jesus' name, amen.

MY PRAYER FOR THE CHAYIL WOMAN

I pray for you, woman of God, that the chayil anointing will be in your life, that virtue, strength, power, might, wealth, riches, business, efficiency, and wisdom—all these things may be stirred inside of you. I pray that you will break out of mediocrity and not use being a woman as an excuse for not advancing in life. I pray that you will see what God has called you to and who God has called you to be, in the name of Jesus.

Thank You, Lord, for letting strength come upon this chayil woman. I thank You, Lord, for the chayil women who have gone before her, all the mothers who have been virtuous, businesslike, strong, efficient, and capable. Thank You, Lord, for every grandmother who exemplified chayil in our lives. Thank You for the chayil woman who is reading this book now. I honor, and I place honor and respect upon her and every chayil woman

*this message may reach. I pray for an increase of
the spirit of might, strength, power, and ability to
come upon their lives.*

Woman of God, if you have ever felt like a doormat and people have walked over you in your life, I break that off of you. You've been controlled. You've been abused. You've been manipulated. You've been taken advantage of by men or society. You can't seem to break out of it. I break the power of every doormat spirit, in the name of Jesus. If you went through a bad marriage, where you felt like a doormat, I break that doormat demon off of your life. If a boyfriend has ever treated you like a doormat, in Jesus' name, I break that demonic power off your life. It is not for the virtuous woman to be trampled and stepped on or walked over. I pray that you'll be strengthened, that God's grace, blessing, and shalom will be released over your life.

I speak might and strength upon you right now in the name of Jesus.

*Thank You, Lord, for doing something new and
fresh in this chayil woman's life. Let this season
in her life be blessed. I pray divine protection
around her. May the blood of Jesus cover her.
May the angel of the Lord surround her. Let no
destruction or premature accident come nigh her
dwelling.*

I decree this over you today, woman of God. I speak shalom, favor, peace, and prosperity over your life. In Jesus' name, amen.

NOTES

Introduction: *Chayil*–Lost in Translation

1. Blue Letter Bible, s.v. *"chayil,"* accessed January 30, 2019, https://www.blueletterbible.org/lang/lexicon/lexicon. cfm?Strongs=H2428&t=KJV.

2. *Merriam-Webster,* s.v. "virtuous," accessed January 30, 2019, https://www.merriam-webster.com/dictionary/ virtuous.

3. Blue Letter Bible, s.v. *"shalowm,"* accessed January 30, 2019, https://www.blueletterbible.org/lang/lexicon/lexicon. cfm?Strongs=H7965&t=KJV.

4. Blue Letter Bible, s.v. *"chayil."*

5. Pat Francis, "The Chayil Woman," Women of Impact Ministries, accessed January 30, 2019, http://www. womenofimpactministries.com/articles/the-chayil-woman-dr-pat-francis.

6. Katharine Bushnell, *God's Word to Women* (n.p.: CreateSpace, 2012).

7. "What Are the Virtues," The Virtues Project, accessed January 30, 2019, https://virtuesproject.com/virtues.html.

8. *Merriam-Webster,* s.v. *"virtue,"* accessed January 30, 2019, https://www.merriam-webster.com/dictionary/virtue.

Chapter 1: A Woman of Valor and Might

1. Blue Letter Bible, s.v. *"Saray,"* accessed January 30, 2019, https://www.blueletterbible.org/lang/lexicon/lexicon. cfm?Strongs=H8297&t=KJV.

2. Blue Letter Bible, s.v. *"sar,"* accessed January 30, 2019, https://www.blueletterbible.org/lang/lexicon/lexicon. cfm?strongs=H8269&t=KJV.

3. Rachel Held Evans, "'Eshet Chayil,' Woman of Valor! (Or, How I Learned the Hebrew Equivalent of 'Carry On, Warrior')," Momastery, April 8, 2013, https://momastery.com/blog/2013/04/08/eshet-chayil-woman-of-valor-or-how-i-learned-the-hebrew-equivalent-of-carry-on-warrior/.

4. Evans, "'Eshet Chayil,' Woman of Valor!"

5. Carol McCleod, "Women of God: 'You Were Created to Be Chayil,'" *Charisma Leader*, September 4, 2015, https://ministrytodaymag.com/life/women/22153-women-of-god-you-were-created-to-be-chayil.

6. Kathi Woodall, "A Chayil Woman," TheChristianPulse.com, October 26, 2012, http://thechristianpulse.com/2012/10/26/a-chayil-woman/.

7. Yael Ziegler, "Ruth: The Woman of Valor," VBM, accessed January 30, 2019, https://etzion.org.il/en/ruth-woman-valor.

8. Michelle McClain-Walters, *The Ruth Anointing* (Lake Mary, FL: Charisma House, 2018).

9. Adapted from Apostle John Eckhardt, "#chayilwomanchallenge: Michelle McClain," Facebook video, June 26, 2018, 9:57 a.m., https://www.facebook.com/apostlejohneckhardt/videos/10156127026306519/.

10. Stella Payton, "Who Is the Chayil Woman?" StellaPayton.com, accessed January 30, 2019, https://stellapayton.com/chayil-woman/.

11. Adapted from Apostle John Eckhardt, "Chayil Woman Challenge, receive the book (electronic) for any donation at PayPal.me/apbooks," Facebook video, June 18, 2018, 10:30 a.m., https://www.facebook.com/apostlejohneckhardt/videos/10156107748891519/.

12. Sophia Ruffin, *Set Free and Delivered* (Lake Mary, FL: Charisma House, 2018).

13. Eckhardt, "Chayil Woman Challenge, receive the book (electronic) for any donation at PayPal.me/apbooks."

14. Adapted from Apostle John Eckhardt, "Chayil Woman Challenge With Valora Cole," Facebook video, June 18, 2018, 8:57 p.m., https://www.facebook.com/apostlejohneckhardt/videos/10156108992236519/.

CHAPTER 2: A WOMAN OF WISDOM AND DISCERNMENT

1. Eckhardt, "#chayilwomanchallenge: Michelle McClain."

2. Adapted from Apostle John Eckhardt, "Chayil Woman Challenge With Kendria Moore," Facebook video, June 21, 2018, 9:02 p.m., https://www.facebook.com/apostlejohneckhardt/videos/10156116679796519/.

3. Eckhardt, "Chayil Woman Challenge With Kendria Moore."

4. Eckhardt, "Chayil Woman Challenge With Kendria Moore."

CHAPTER 3: A WOMAN OF SUBSTANCE AND WEALTH

1. Blue Letter Bible, s.v. "*chayil.*"

2. *Strong's Exhaustive Concordance*, s.v. "*chayil*," Bible Study Tools, accessed January 30, 2019, https://www.biblestudytools.com/lexicons/hebrew/kjv/chayil.html.

3. *English Oxford Living Dictionaries*, s.v. "efficient," accessed January 30, 2019, https://en.oxforddictionaries.com/definition/efficient.

4. Eckhardt, "Chayil Woman Challenge, receive the book (electronic) for any donation at PayPal.me/apbooks."

5. Blue Letter Bible, s.v. "*koach*," accessed January 30, 2019, https://www.blueletterbible.org/lang/lexicon/lexicon.cfm?Strongs=H3581&t=KJV.

6. Blue Letter Bible, s.v. "*koach*."

7. Eckhardt, "#chayilwomanchallenge: Michelle McClain."

CHAPTER 4: A WOMAN OF WORSHIP, PRAYER, AND FAITH

1. Pamela Hardy, *Dance: The Higher Call* (n.p.: Reignaissance Publications, 2015); *Unlocking Your Prophetic Destiny* (n.p.: Reignaissance Publications, 2017); *Far Above Rubies: The Power of Christ's Virtue in You* (Plano, TX: Eagles Global Books, 2018).

2. Blue Letter Bible, s.v. "*chuwl*," accessed January 30, 2019, https://www.blueletterbible.org/lang/lexicon/lexicon.cfm?strongs=H2342&t=KJV.

3. Adapted from Apostle John Eckhardt, "Chayil Woman Challenge With Dr. Pamela Hardy," Facebook video, June 19, 2018, 9:59 a.m., https://www.facebook.com/apostlejohneckhardt/videos/10156110218501519/.

4. Eckhardt, "Chayil Woman Challenge With Dr. Pamela Hardy."

5. Eckhardt, "Chayil Woman Challenge With Dr. Pamela Hardy."

6. LaJun M. Cole and Valora Shaw-Cole, *Plug Into the Power of Prayer and Prophetic Intercession* (n.p.: CreateSpace, 2014).

7. Valora Shaw-Cole, *I Am Fearless Journal* (n.p.: CreateSpace, 2016).

8. Eckhardt, "Chayil Woman Challenge With Valora Cole."

9. Eckhardt, "Chayil Woman Challenge With Valora Cole." This declaration was adapted from Urban Dictionary, s.v.

"fearless," June 17, 2009, https://www.urbandictionary.com/define.php?term=Fearless.

CHAPTER 5: A WOMAN OF RARE AND NOBLE CHARACTER

1. TOW Project, "Lady Wisdom in Street Clothes," Theology of Work, accessed January 31, 2019, https://www.theologyofwork.org/key-topics/women-and-work-in-the-old-testament/lady-wisdom-in-street-clothes-proverbs-31.

2. Eckhardt, "#chayilwomanchallenge: Michelle McClain."

CHAPTER 6: A WOMAN OF POWER AND INFLUENCE

1. Michelle McClain-Walters, *The Deborah Anointing* (Lake Mary, FL: Charisma House, 2015).

2. Eckhardt, "#chayilwomanchallenge: Michelle McClain."

3. "Investment by Women, and in Them, Is Growing," *Economist*, March 8, 2018, https://www.economist.com/finance-and-economics/2018/03/08/investment-by-women-and-in-them-is-growing.

4. Adapted from Apostle John Eckhardt, "Chayil Challenge With Yolanda Stith," Facebook video, June 22, 2018, 10:13 a.m., https://www.facebook.com/apostlejohneckhardt/videos/10156117793111519/.

5. Eckhardt, "Chayil Challenge With Yolanda Stith."

6. Eckhardt, "Chayil Challenge With Yolanda Stith."

7. Eckhardt, "Chayil Challenge With Yolanda Stith."